ALSO BY DAVID CLARK
with MARY BUFFETT

The Warren Buffett Stock Portfolio

Warren Buffett and the Art of Stock Arbitrage

Warren Buffett's Management Secrets

Warren Buffett and the Interpretation of Financial Statements

The Tao of Warren Buffett

The New Buffettology

The Buffettology Workbook

Buffettology

THE TAO OF CHARLIE MUNGER

A COMPILATION OF QUOTES
FROM BERKSHIRE HATHAWAY'S
VICE CHAIRMAN ON LIFE, BUSINESS,
AND THE PURSUIT OF WEALTH

WITH COMMENTARY BY
DAVID CLARK

SCRIBNER
New York London Toronto Sydney New Delhi

SCRIBNER

An Imprint of Simon & Schuster, Inc.

1230 Avenue of the Americas

New York, NY 10020

First Scribner hardcover edition January 2017

SCRIBNER and design are registered trademarks of The Gale Group, Inc., used under license by Simon & Schuster, Inc., the publisher of this work.

For information about special discounts for bulk purchases, please contact Simon & Schuster Special Sales at 1-866-506-1949 or business@simonandschuster.com.

The Simon & Schuster Speakers Bureau can bring authors to your live event. For more information or to book an event, contact the Simon & Schuster Speakers Bureau at 1-866-248-3049 or visit our website at www.simonspeakers.com.

Interior design by Kyle Kabel

Manufactured in the United States of America

13 15 17 19 20 18 16 14 12

Library of Congress Cataloging-in-Publication Data is available.

ISBN 978-1-5011-5334-1

ISBN 978-1-5011-5335-8 (ebook)

This book is dedicated to Richard Saunders and his merry band of troublemakers. Never have so many owed so few so much.

CONTENTS

—

SOURCE NOTE

The Charlie Munger quotes I chose to include in this book come from a variety of sources that are available on the Internet, among them newspapers, magazines, journals, speeches, books, blogs, quote websites, and other websites. Quotes from company annual meetings come from the online reports posted by attendees and do not necessarily represent a word-for-word recitation of the statements at the meeting. I have identified the sources with their corresponding websites in the back of the book for those of you who wish to continue reading about the very fascinating, and ever interesting, Charlie Munger.

THE TAO OF
CHARLIE
MUNGER

INTRODUCTION

In the chronicles of American financial history Charlie Munger will be seen as the proverbial enigma wrapped in a paradox—he is both a mystery and a contradiction at the same time. Warren Buffett said, "Charlie's most important architectural feat was the design of today's Berkshire. The blueprint he gave me was simple: Forget what you know about buying fair businesses at wonderful prices; instead, buy wonderful businesses at fair prices. . . . Consequently, Berkshire has been built to Charlie's blueprint. My role has been that of general contractor, with the CEOs of Berkshire's subsidiaries doing the real work as subcontractors."

How is it that Charlie—who trained as a meteorologist and a lawyer and never took a single college course in economics, marketing, finance, or accounting—became one of the greatest business and investing geniuses of the twentieth and twenty-first centuries? Therein lies the mystery.

Charlie was born in Omaha, Nebraska, on January 1, 1924, in the midst of the Roaring Twenties. The radio and airplane were the cutting-edge technologies of the day. The financier Bernard Baruch was the king of Wall Street. And everyone was getting rich investing in stocks. Charlie's father was one of Omaha's leading business attorneys, and his roster of clients included many of the state's business elite. Charlie spent much of his youth reading—the television and video games of his day—and that is where he discovered a larger world than the idyllic, but very parochial, neighborhood of Dundee, where Warren Buffett's family also lived. The two boys attended the same grade school and high school, though seven years apart in age. In fact, one of Charlie's first jobs was working for Warren's grandfather at the Buffett neighborhood grocery store—which is still standing in the heart of old Dundee.

Charlie was introduced to the world of business at the Buffett grocery store. He learned about taking inventory, stocking shelves, pleasing customers, the importance of showing up on time for work, how to get along with others while accomplishing a joint task, and, of course, running the cash register, where money, the lifeblood of the business, flowed.

Omaha in the 1930s had distinct ethnic immigrant neighborhoods: Italian, Greek, African American, Irish, French, Czech, Russian, and even Chinese. Many immigrants worked for the Union Pacific Railroad and meatpacking plants whose operations were centered in Omaha. Charlie went to public school with the children of those immigrants and as a result developed an appreciation not only of their cultures but also of their commercial aptitude and willingness to work unbelievably hard to give their children a better life.

Charlie often brings up the horrors of the Great Depression at Berkshire Hathaway annual meetings as a reminder of just how bad things can get. But Omaha didn't suffer like other parts of the United States during the Great Depression, in part because it was the crossroads of two major railroads, the Union Pacific and the Burlington, and also because it was home to the Union Stock Yards, the second largest in the world. With this convergence of livestock and transportation, Omaha attracted the big meatpacking companies, which established processing plants in South Omaha. America may have been in a great depression, but it still had to eat, and as many as twenty thousand pigs, sheep, and cattle arrived in Omaha every day. Those animals needed to be slaughtered, butchered, packed, and shipped to other parts of the country. The stockyard generated lots of economic activity even during hard times.

The Kiewit construction company, today one of North America's largest building companies, was founded in Omaha. The company's first big job was constructing the Livestock Exchange building for the Union Stock Yards. (Peter Kiewit had a huge influence on both Charlie and Warren, and today Berkshire's home office is in Kiewit Plaza.) Charlie learned about the business dealings of some of Omaha's most prominent businessmen from his father, who represented both the Hitchcock family, who owned the town's leading newspaper, and the Kountze family, who owned the largest bank.

After high school, seventeen-year-old Charlie enrolled in the University of Michigan to study mathematics. He turned nineteen a year after Pearl Harbor, dropped out of college, and joined the US Army Air Corps. The army sent him to Caltech, in Pasadena, California, to study meteorology. There he learned the difference between cumulus and cirrus clouds and fell in love with the sunny Southern California weather.

While the teenage Warren Buffett was busy learning about odds and probability at the Ak-Sar-Ben horse-racing track—a short bike ride from his Omaha home—Charlie Munger was learning this important investment skill while playing poker with his army buddies. That's where he learned to fold his hand when the odds were against him and bet heavy when the odds were with him, a strategy he later adapted to investing.

After the war Charlie, who did not have an undergrad degree, applied to Harvard Law School, his father's alma mater. He was rejected. After a phone call from Harvard Law's retired dean, who was a Nebraskan and family friend, he was admitted. Charlie excelled in his law studies and graduated magna cum laude in 1948. He has never forgotten the importance of having friends in high places.

After law school Charlie moved back to Los Angeles, where he joined a prestigious corporate law firm. He learned a lot about business from handling the affairs of Twentieth Century–Fox, a mining operation in the Mojave Desert, and many real estate deals. During that time he was also the director of an International Harvester dealership, where he first learned how hard it is to fix a struggling business. The dealership was a volume business that required a lot of capital to pay for its costly inventory, most of it financed with a bank loan. A couple of bad seasons, and the carrying costs on the inventory start to destroy the business. But if the company cut its inventory to lower the carrying costs, it wouldn't have had anything to sell, which meant that customers would seek out a competing dealership that did have inventory. It was a tough business with lots of problems and no easy solutions.

Charlie thought a lot about business during that time. He made a habit of asking people what was the best business they knew of. He longed to join the rich elite clientele his silk-stocking law firm served. He decided that each day he would devote one hour of his time at the office to work on his own real estate projects, and by doing so he completed five. He has said that the first million dollars he put together was the hardest money he ever earned. It was also during that period that he realized he would never become really rich practicing law; he'd have to find something else.

In the summer of 1959, while in Omaha to settle his

father's estate, he met two old friends for lunch at the Omaha Club, a wood-paneled, private downtown club where businessmen lunched in the afternoon and drank and smoked cigars in the evening. The two men had decided to bring along a friend of theirs who was running a partnership they had invested in and whom they thought Charlie would enjoy meeting, a young man by the name of Warren Buffett.

By all accounts it was a case of instant mutual attraction. Warren started by launching into his standard diatribe about the investment genius of Benjamin Graham. Charlie knew about Graham, and immediately the two began to talk about businesses and stocks. The conversation became so intense that Charlie and Warren barely noticed when their two friends got up to leave. That was the beginning of a long and very profitable relationship—a bromance in the making—and over the next couple of days they couldn't see enough of each other. One night over dinner Charlie asked if Warren thought it would be possible for Charlie to open an investment partnership like Warren's in California. Warren said he couldn't see any reason why not.

After Charlie returned to California, he and Warren talked several times a week on the phone over the next couple of years. And in 1962 Charlie finally started an investment partnership with an old poker buddy who was also a trader on the Pacific Coast Stock Exchange. He also started a new law firm, Munger, Tolles, Hills and Woods.

Within three years he stopped practicing law to focus on investing full-time.

Charlie's investment partnership was different from Warren's, in that he was willing to take on a lot of debt to do some of his trades. He was particularly fond of stock arbitrage. One arbitrage deal involved British Columbia Power, a company that was being taken over by the Canadian government. The takeover price was $22 a share. BCP was selling for $19 a share. Thinking that the deal would eventually go through at $22 a share, Charlie bought all the shares of BCP he could get his hands on and ended up putting all of the partnership's money, all of his own money, and all that he could borrow into BCP. The trade worked out—BCP was taken over at $22 a share—and Charlie made out like a bandit.

In the mid-1960s Charlie and Warren were busy scouring over the Pink Sheets (a pre-Internet daily publication of the prices of OTC stocks printed on pink paper) looking for a bargain price on a good company. One of the companies they found was Blue Chip Stamp. Blue Chip was a trading stamp company; other businesses would buy trading stamps from Blue Chip to give them to their customers, who would then redeem them for prizes that Blue Chip was offering. Think of it as an early form of a rewards program. What made the company interesting to Charlie was that Blue Chip had a pool of money called a "float" that was created by the lag time between its selling the stamps and the customer's redeeming them. What made Blue Chip's stock attractively priced was the fact that the US government had filed an antitrust action against the company. Charlie, as a lawyer, thought the lawsuit would be resolved in favor of Blue Chip—which it was. Charlie—through his partnership—and Warren—through Berkshire—eventually took control of the company, and Charlie became its chairman. By the late 1970s the float at Blue Chip had grown to approximately $100 million, money that Charlie and Warren could invest.

Blue Chip's business model eventually became obsolete, and its sales slowly declined over the years, from $126 million in sales in 1970 to $1.5 million in 1990. But in its heyday, under Charlie's direction, Blue Chip used its surplus capital to purchase 100% of See's Candies and 80% of a finance company called Wesco, which owned a savings and loan. Just as Warren had taken capital out of Berkshire's failing textile operation to buy a thriving insurance company, National Indemnity, Charlie took the excess capital out of Blue Chip Stamp and invested it in profitable businesses. Eventually Blue Chip Stamp was merged into Berkshire Hathaway.

In 1968 Charlie teamed up with Warren and David "Sandy" Gottesman, who ran the investment firm First Manhattan, to form Diversified Retailing Company. DRC acquired the Baltimore-based department store Hochschild Kohn for $12 million. Half of the acquisition was financed with a bank loan. Hochschild Kohn was bought at a bargain price, but it had no competitive advantage and was constantly having to spend precious capital keeping up with the competition. Charlie and the others quickly learned how hard the retail clothing business really is. Unlike the jewelry or carpet business, where the inventory never depreciates, in retail clothing the entire inventory becomes obsolete with the changing of every season. After three years of dismal results they sold Hochschild Kohn.

During that time Charlie started seeing the advantages of investing in better businesses that didn't have big capital requirements and did have lots of free cash that could be reinvested in expanding operations or buying new businesses.

From 1961 to 1969 Charlie's investment partnership showed an amazing average annual return of 37.1%. But the crash in 1973–74 hurt him, and when he closed the fund in 1975 it had $10 million in assets and showed an average annual rate of return of 24.3% for the fourteen years it was in operation. What is interesting is that in the final years of the fund Charlie was running a highly concentrated portfolio, the holding in Blue Chip Stamp alone accounting for 61% of the fund's investments. He has never been a fan of diversification as an investment strategy.

One of the investment decisions that Charlie's partnership made in 1972 was to team up with the investor Rick Guerin and take a controlling interest in a closed-end investment fund called Fund of Letters, which they quickly renamed the New America Fund. When the partnership liquidated the partners received shares in the New America Fund, which Guerin ran and for which Charlie picked the investments. In 1977 New America Fund bought the Daily Journal Corporation for $2.5 million, and Charlie became its chairman. The Daily Journal Corporation is a California publishing company that publishes newspapers and magazines, including the *Los Angeles Daily Journal* and the *San Francisco Daily Journal*. When Guerin and Charlie dissolved the New America Fund, its shareholders received shares in the Daily Journal Corporation and the company became a publicly traded OTC stock. Many of today's Daily Journal shareholders have literally been with Charlie since the days of his original investment partnership, more than forty years ago.

In 1979 Charlie became Berkshire Hathaway's first vice chairman. In 1983 Blue Chip Stamp merged with Berkshire Hathaway and Charlie took over as chairman of Wesco. It was from those two positions that Charlie would help Warren make the investment and management decisions that would take Berkshire Hathaway from a net income of $148 million and a stock price of $1,272 a share in 1984 to a net income of approximately $24 billion and a stock price of $210,000 a share in 2016.

Today, at ninety-two, Charlie is vice chairman of Berkshire Hathaway, a company with a market capitalization of $362 billion, as well as the chairman of the Daily Journal Corporation, and his personal fortune now exceeds $2 billion.

Warren, in summing up Charlie's impact on his investment style over the last fifty-seven years, said, "Charlie shoved me in the direction of not just buying bargains, as Ben Graham had taught me. This was the real impact that he had on me. It took a powerful force to move me on from Graham's limiting view. It was the power of Charlie's mind."

PART I

–

CHARLIE'S THOUGHTS ON SUCCESSFUL INVESTING

FAST MONEY

–

"The desire to get rich fast is pretty dangerous."

–

Trying to get rich fast is dangerous because we have to gamble on the short-term price direction of some stock or other asset. There are a huge number of people trying to do the same thing, many of whom are much better informed than we are. The short-term price direction of any security or derivative contract is subject to all kinds of wild price swings due to events that have nothing to do with the actual long-term value of the underlying business or asset. Last but not least, there is the problem of leverage: to get rich quickly, one often has to use leverage/debt to amplify small price swings into really huge gains. If things go against us, they can also turn into really large losses. So we take a leveraged position in a stock, thinking we are going to hit it big; then something terrible like 9/11 happens, the stock market tanks, and we get wiped out. In his early days, Charlie did use a lot of leverage on his stock arbitrage investments, but as he got older he saw the grave danger he was putting himself in and now passionately avoids using debt and bets only on the long-term economics of a business, not the short-term price swings of its stock price.

CIRCLE OF COMPETENCE

—

"Knowing what you don't know is more useful than being brilliant."

—

What Charlie is saying here is that we should become conscious of what we don't know and use that knowledge to stay away from investing in businesses we don't understand.

At the height of the bull market bubble in technology stocks in the late 1990s, many very brilliant people were seduced into investing in Internet stocks. Charlie realized that he didn't understand the new Internet businesses, which were outside what he calls his circle of competence, so he and Berkshire avoided them completely. Most of Wall Street thought he had lost his touch. But when the bubble finally burst and the companies' stock prices fell, fortunes were lost, and it was Charlie who was left looking brilliant.

AVOID BEING AN IDIOT

–

"People are trying to be smart—all I am trying to do is not to be idiotic, but it's harder than most people think."

–

Charlie's investment philosophy is predicated on the theory that a shortsighted stock market will sometimes underprice a company's shares relative to the long-term economic value of the company. When that happens, he buys into the company, holds it for the long term, and lets the underlying economics of the business eventually lift the stock price. The only thing he has to be careful about is not doing something stupid, which in his case are mostly errors of omission, such as not acting when he sees a good investment or buying too little of it when the opportunity presents itself. Which is actually harder to do than one might think.

WALKING AWAY

–

"Life, in part, is like a poker game, wherein you have to learn to quit sometimes when holding a much-loved hand—you must learn to handle mistakes and new facts that change the odds."

–

Charlie experienced this with the home mortgage lender Freddie Mac. When Berkshire bought shares in Freddie Mac in the 1980s, it was a very well run, conservatively managed, profitable enterprise involved in the mortgage business. As time went on, Freddie's management branched out into a new line of business in which they were using their quasi-governmental status to aggressively borrow short-term money and then lend it out long term—the same financial equation that eventually put Lehman Brothers into bankruptcy. Seeing the dramatic increase in risk and the change in the attitude of Freddie Mac's management, Berkshire sold its much-loved investment at a profit in 1999. By 2008 Freddie Mac was in receivership (a kind of bankruptcy), the old management had been fired, and the stock was worth a tiny faction of what it had been when Berkshire sold its shares. Charlie knows when to hold 'em, knows when to fold 'em, and knows when to walk away.

EASY SHOOTING

—

"My idea of shooting a fish in a barrel is draining the barrel first."

—

Sometimes the shortsighted stock market serves up an investment opportunity that is so obvious it is hard to resist. This usually happens when there is a stock market panic and investors are fleeing any and all investments, even the ones with great long-term economics working in their favor. This fleeing of investors is the draining of the barrel—stock prices drop, which makes it easier for Charlie to see the fish: underpriced great businesses.

REVELATION

—

"Once we'd gotten over the hurdle of recognizing that a thing could be a bargain based on quantitative measures that would have horrified Graham, we started thinking about better businesses."

—

Benjamin Graham was the dean of value investing. He was also Warren Buffett's teacher and mentor, and in his world value investing meant buying a stock at below its intrinsic value—which to Graham meant half of book value or at a very low price-to-earnings ratio. One could readily do that in the period of 1933 to 1965 if one worked hard enough at finding those kinds of bargains. The problem with Graham's investment philosophy was that it required an investor to sell the stock once it rose to its intrinsic value. There was no such thing as owning a company for twenty years or longer and letting the underlying economics of the business grow the company and lift the stock price.

Charlie and Warren realized that some businesses have exceptional economics working in their favor that will cause their intrinsic value to increase over time. The common stock of these amazing companies really is a kind of equity bond that has an increasing rate of interest (earnings) attached to it. For example: When Berkshire started buying

Coca-Cola stock in 1988 (figures are adjusted for splits), the company had earnings of $0.18 a share and was growing its per share earnings at a rate of approximately 16% a year. Berkshire paid approximately $3.24 a share, which equates to a P/E ratio of 18, way too high for the likes of Graham. But Charlie and Warren could see something that Graham couldn't: that the long-term economics of the business made it a bargain at a P/E ratio of 18. They saw Coca-Cola's stock as a kind of equity bond, which was paying an initial rate of return of 5.55% ($0.18 EPS divided by $3.24 = 5.55%), which would continue to increase as Coke's per share earnings continued to grow; and that over the long term, the market would advance Coke's share price as the company's earnings grew.

So how did Berkshire do? Its $1.299 billion original investment in Coke in 1988, over the last twenty-seven years, has grown to be worth $17.184 billion, giving Berkshire an average annual compounding rate of return of 10.04% for the twenty-seven years, which doesn't even include all the dividends that it received in that time period. In 2015 alone, Coca-Cola paid to Berkshire $528 million in dividends, giving Berkshire a current annual dividend rate of return of 40% on its initial investment of $1.299 billion. Over the next five years Coca-Cola will pay Berkshire approximately $2.64 billion in dividends. Things really do go better with a Coke, including our money.

GRAHAM'S ERROR

—

"Ben Graham had a lot to learn as an investor. His ideas of how to value companies were all shaped by how the Great Crash and the Depression almost destroyed him. . . . It left him with an aftermath of fear for the rest of his life, and all his methods were designed to keep that at bay."

—

The crash of October 29, 1929, was hard on Graham, and the ensuing crash in 1932 was devastating. After the crash of 1929, stock prices started to rise, increasing by 30% by 1931. The crash of 1932 was completely unexpected and the worst in the twentieth century. It drove stock prices down by 89%. If you had $1,000 invested in the Dow on September 3, 1929, it would have gone down to $109 by July 8, 1932.

To protect himself in the future, Graham developed the concept of the margin of safety, a quantitative approach to valuation that he adapted out of bond analysis and the fear of bankruptcy. He looked for companies that were selling on a per share basis for less than their book value. Thus he developed the buying-the-whole-business approach. He'd value the whole business at, say $10 million, and then he would figure out what the company was selling for on the stock market. If it had a million shares outstanding and was selling at $6 a share, he could see that the stock market was valuing the entire company at $6 million. But its intrinsic value was $10 million, which gave him a margin of safety of $4 million. So even if the stock market crashed, the company's $10 million intrinsic value would eventually pull its stock price back up.

Where this hurt him was that his system required him to sell an investment once it reached its intrinsic value. There was no such thing as holding a stock for thirty or forty years, as Charlie and Warren do. If he had bought Berkshire Hathaway in 1974, when it was selling at half its book value, he would have sold it in 1980, when it was selling above book value. There would have been no riding it to $210,000 a share in 2016. His investment philosophy was designed to make him money and to protect him from losses, but it also stopped him from ever benefiting from the compounding effect that a great business can generate over a period of ten, twenty, or more years.

SITTING ON YOUR ASS

—

"Sit on your ass investing. You're paying less to brokers, you're listening to less nonsense, and if it works, the tax system gives you an extra one, two, or three percentage points per annum."

—

This important investment philosophy assumes that one is better off buying a business with exceptional business economics working in its favor and holding it for many years than engaging in a lot of buying and selling, trying to anticipate market trends. Constantly buying and selling means constantly being taxed. If one holds an investment for twenty years there is only one tax to pay, which, according to Charlie, equates to an extra 1 to 3 extra percentage points of profit per year.

Though the 3 extra percentage points may not seem like much, consider this: a million-dollar investment compounding at 4% a year will have grown in year twenty to $2,191,123. Add three percentage points (4% + 3% = 7%), so that the million-dollar investment is compounding for twenty years at 7%, and you will end up with a sum of $3,869,684 in the twentieth year.

Charlie knows that time is a good friend to a business that has exceptional economics working in its favor, but for a mediocre business time can be a curse.

THE DAWNING OF WISDOM

—

"Acknowledging what you don't know is the dawning of wisdom."

—

The smarter we get, the more we realize how little we actually do know. By acknowledging what we don't know, we are putting ourselves into a position to learn more; thus, the dawning of wisdom.

In Charlie's world of investing there is what he calls a "circle of competence," which consists of all the companies he is capable of understanding and valuing. But it also includes all the companies outside the circle that he doesn't understand and is unable to value. By acknowledging what he doesn't know, he can either avoid an investment or learn more about the business and see if he can understand it to the point that he can value it, which would put it within his circle of competence. Over the course of Charlie's life he has increased his circle of competence to include the insurance business, banking, newspapers, television, candy companies, airlines, the toolmaking business, boot makers, underwear manufacturers, power companies, and investment banking. Charlie's road to all this wisdom began by acknowledging what he didn't know and then doing something about it.

ANALYSTS

—

*"In the corporate world, if you have analysts, due
diligence, and no horse sense, you've just described hell."*

—

I think what Charlie is saying is that when analysts from a ratings
company such as Moody's Corporation issue a new rating on a bond,
while being paid millions by the Wall Street investment bank that
requested the rating, we should probably be a little suspicious. The
ratings companies have a very strong incentive to provide the investment banks with the highest ratings possible for their financial
products—even if said products might not really deserve such a good
rating. Which is exactly what helped create the housing bubble, the
subsequent stock market crash, and the Great Recession of 2007–09.
The problem we face today is that the financial incentive for the
ratings companies to paint a rosy picture for the investment banks
still exists. Fool me once, shame on you; fool me twice, shame on me.

A MISPRICED GAMBLE

—

"You're looking for a mispriced gamble. That's what investing is. And you have to know enough to know whether the gamble is mispriced. That's value investing."

—

A company is a mispriced gamble when the price of the stock is out of sync with the company's long-term future economics. This mispricing can be on the upside, meaning that the stock price significantly overvalues the long-term prospects of the business. Or it may be on the downside, meaning that the stock price greatly undervalues the long-term prospects of the company. As the stock price starts to drop, the business begins to become mispriced on the downside, in relation to the company's long-term future prospects. The lower the share price goes, the more mispriced it becomes. This is when the odds are in your favor and it is time to buy. You get great value for your money by buying into a company with great long-term economics working in its favor whose share price is mispriced on the downside. Why does this mispricing phenomenon occur? Because of the shortsighted nature of the institutions—primarily mutual funds and hedge funds—that are the dominant players in the stock market and that are concerned only with the direction in which a company's share price is headed over the next six months. Charlie, by contrast, is concerned only about where a company's underlying economics are headed over the next ten years. It is the discrepancy between the two that creates his mispriced gamble—his buying opportunity.

DIVERSIFICATION

–

"This worshipping at the altar of diversification, I think that is really crazy."

–

Diversification is a way to protect financial consultants and stock brokers from ever looking really bad, but it also stops them from looking really good as well. What happens with broad diversification—holding a portfolio of, say, fifty or more different stocks—is that the winners will be canceled out by the losers, just as the losers will be canceled out by the winners. Diversification creates a situation that basically mimics the market or an index fund. An adviser who counsels diversification never looks very good or very bad, just average.

Charlie discovered that if we invest in companies that have great economics working in their favor, at a reasonable price, we can bring the number of companies we own down to ten or fewer and still be protected against an unexpected business failure, and have good growth of our portfolio over a ten- to twenty-year period. As the saying goes, too much diversification, and we end up with a zoo. It's much easier to keep a sharp eye on our basket if there are only ten eggs in it.

WHEN TO BET HEAVILY

—

"You should remember that good ideas are rare—when the odds are greatly in your favor, bet heavily."

—

Even when a great investment is lying right in front of most investors, they will only nibble at it. Which is not the way to make the big bucks. When are the odds in our favor? When some macroeconomic event causes stock prices to collapse, Charlie buys as much as possible. Remember, in Charlie's world, as stock prices fall, the odds become more in our favor, provided we invest in companies with good long-term economics working in their favor. When that happens, Charlie recommends that we bet big!

THE HERD

—

"Mimicking the herd invites regression to the mean."

—

Charlie is telling us that if we invest in an index fund, we will do no better than the average investor. We will never excel beyond the average, and average can also mean losing. If we buy into an index fund at the height of a bull market and the market tanks, it is possible we might lose money for a number of years. In Charlie's world one buys as others are selling, which is hard to do if one is running with the herd.

FORESIGHT

–

"I've never been able to predict accurately. I don't make money predicting accurately. We just tend to get into good businesses and stay there."

–

Charlie is no good at forecasting the future, be it the weather, elections, the economy, or the stock market—especially the stock market. All that banter in the financial press about what is going to happen in the stock market is mindless noise to him. He's just a man looking for a good business he can buy at a fair price. However, the one thing he can predict is that the stock market will have moments of wild exuberance and high stock prices, usually followed by bouts of severe depression and much lower stock prices. Can he predict with accuracy when these events will happen? No. But he does know they will happen—he just has to have the patience to let them happen.

FINANCIAL CRISIS
EQUALS OPPORTUNITY

–

*"If you, like me, lived through 1973–74 or even the early
1990s . . . there was a waiting list to get OUT of the
country club—that's when you know things are tough.
If you live long enough, you'll see it."*

–

The United States experienced an economic recession in 1973–74,
and again in the early 1990s, which brought on unemployment and
crashing stock prices. The 1973–74 recession was caused by a rise
in oil prices. It lasted twenty-four months and caused the Dow Jones
Industrial Average to lose 45% of its value. The early '90s recession
was also caused by rising oil prices, but also by overbuilding in the
1980s, which caused a slump in office building construction. The
recession lasted eight months and caused the Dow to lose 18% of
its value.

In 2001, six years before the Great Recession set in, Charlie knew
that there would eventually be another great economic upheaval. He
was correct. In 2007–09 the economy collapsed, stock prices fell,
and the Dow lost 54% of its value. How did he know that would
happen? He knows that cyclical financial crises are just in the nature
of capitalism. That a heavily leveraged banking system, when mixed

with speculative frenzy, can create massively unstable investment bubbles, which inevitably burst and bring the entire economy down.

I would be amiss if I didn't point out that random recessions/crashes are programed into Charlie's buying strategy. Both Charlie and Warren let cash pile up, waiting for a recession/crash, even if it means getting low rates of return on their cash holdings as they wait for the inevitable. When the crash hits, they make their purchases. In the 1990 recession, bank stocks took a big hit, which Berkshire used as a buying opportunity to acquire 5 million shares of Wells Fargo bank at a cost of $289 million. Today, those 5 million shares, thanks to stock splits, have grown to 40 million shares that are now worth approximately $1.9 billion. Which gives Berkshire, excluding dividends, a 7.5% compounding annual rate of return for the twenty-six-year period. But the icing on the cake is that Berkshire's original $289 million investment is now earning it $59.2 million a year in dividends—which equates to an annual dividend payout of 20.4% on its original investment. As Charlie has said many times, it wasn't brains that made him so rich, it was temperament.

17

CASH IS KEY

—

"The way to get rich is to keep $10 million in your checking account in case a good deal comes along."

—

Charlie advocates keeping $10 million in cash, and Berkshire keeps $72 billion sitting around in cash, waiting for the right deal to show up. The lousy return their cash balances are getting is a trade-off—poor initial rate of return in exchange for years of high returns from finding excellent businesses selling at a fair price. This is an element of the Munger investment equation that is almost always misunderstood. Why? Because most investors cannot image that sitting on a large pool of cash year after year, waiting for the right investment, could possibly be a winning investment strategy, let alone one that would make them superrich.

A DEMORALIZED GENERATION

–

"Thanks to the early 1930s and the behavior of the capitalists in the robber-baron days . . . stocks yielded dividends that were twice as much as the interest rates on bonds. It was a wonderful period to be buying stocks. We profited from others' demoralization from the previous generation."

–

The crashes of 1929 and 1932 decimated stock prices so badly that it took until 1954 for the Dow Jones Industrial Average to return to its 1929 high. Many people lost their entire fortunes. That soured the investing public on common stocks for almost thirty years. Many of the companies whose stock prices were devastated by the crash returned to profitability by the 1940s, but no one was interested in owning their shares.

To attract investors, companies had to pay dividends that were almost twice what bonds were paying. Charlie and Warren cut their investment teeth on buying those companies, which were paying a substantial dividend and often selling at prices below their book values. As investing in common stocks came back into vogue in the late 1950s and early '60s, the companies' stock prices started to rise, making Charlie and Warren multimillionaires.

By the late 1960s the bargains started disappearing, and by 1972 they were pretty much gone; the bull market had overpriced everything.

PATIENCE

–

"I succeeded because I have a long attention span."

–

Patience is a virtue, and it is also an asset in the investment game. Most people think that means patiently sitting on some investment forever, waiting for its value to go up. In Charlie's world it also means sitting patiently on a pile of cash waiting for some great business's stock price to get beaten down. And it means having the patience to stay focused on looking for a great company selling at a fair price. The intense focusing skills it takes to become a lawyer or a doctor are the same skills it takes to become a great investor.

STOCK PRICES

—

"It is an unfortunate fact that great and foolish excess can come into prices of common stocks in the aggregate. They are valued partly like bonds, based on roughly rational projections of use value in producing future cash. But they are also valued partly like Rembrandt paintings, purchased mostly because their prices have gone up, so far."

—

This is very interesting, and it belies several of the underlying thought processes that have made Charlie so incredibly wealthy.

First, the bond piece: Some companies—not all, but some—have businesses that create fairly consistent earnings and earnings growth. Charlie and Warren believe that the common stock in those special businesses can be valued like bonds. So if a company is earning $1 a share and the stock is selling at $10 a share, one can argue that the stock is like an equity bond that is earning 10%. If the company's earnings are growing at 5% a year, our two boys can argue that they just bought an "equity bond" that is earning 10% a year and growing at 5% a year. They think of it as an "equity bond" with an expanding rate of return, which, over time, lifts the underlying value of the company and thus its share price.

The Rembrandt painting analogy refers to the fact that the market for old masters' paintings is driven by demand, and demand is often determined by how quickly selling prices are rising or falling. The same thing can happen in stocks; a fast-rising price can attract more buyers, just as a fast-falling stock price can attract more sellers. When an asset bubble bursts and demand for equity instruments evaporates, people sell their Rembrandts and stocks for whatever they can get for them because they are desperately in need of cash. For Charlie and Warren, the time to buy the "equity bonds" of a wonderful company is when everyone else is trying to sell their Rembrandts.

EBITDA

—

"I think that, every time you see the word EBITDA, you should substitute the word 'bullshit earnings.'"

—

EBITDA stands for "earnings before interest, taxes, depreciation, and amortization." Charlie considers interest, depreciation, and taxes to be very real expenses that have to be paid. Interest and taxes have to be paid in the current year. Depreciation is a cost that has to be paid at a later date—for example, when a plant and equipment eventually need replacing. That eventual replacement is a capital cost. And capital costs can destroy what otherwise appears to be a really great business. According to Charlie, if we use EBITDA to determine the earnings of a company, we will get an unrealistic view of the company's true economic nature.

DANGERS OF
FINANCE COMPANIES

–

"Where you have complexity, by nature you can have fraud and mistakes. . . . This will always be true of financial companies, including ones run by governments. If you want accurate numbers from financial companies, you're in the wrong world."

–

How complex are financial companies? Charlie says that it is almost impossible to know if one has gone astray until the day a company collapses. Just look at Lehman Brothers: one year it is trading at $65 a share and is the toast of Wall Street; a year later it is in bankruptcy. The same for the insurance giant AIG and the great investment banking house Merrill Lynch: one year they are considered two of the soundest financial firms in the world, the next year they are begging for money from the government.

What makes financial companies so complex? Derivatives make it possible to hide risk from the prying eyes of regulators and investment analysts. With AIG it was impossible to see all the credit default swaps it had written on subprime mortgages, because it never set aside any reserves to cover its losses. That meant the company's risk exposure was hidden from the investing public. You could have read Lehman

Brothers' annual report a hundred times and never realized that it was borrowing hundreds of billions of dollars short term and lending them out long term to finance subprime mortgages that they then used as collateral to borrow even more money. A commercial bank might be using derivatives to take a massively speculative position in the currency markets, but accounting regulations are such that the position would be impossible to ascertain—until the company loses several hundred million dollars and we read about it in the financial press. Charlie's rule for financial firms is really simple: what looks good on the outside may be seriously rotten on the inside.

OVERCONFIDENCE

—

"Smart people aren't exempt from professional disasters from overconfidence."

—

Here Charlie is referring to the collapse of Long-Term Capital Management, which was a hedge fund set up by the famed Wall Street bond trader John Meriwether in the late 1990s. Meriwether brought together some the smartest people from Wall Street and academia, including PhDs in mathematics and economics, several of whom who were Nobel laureates. Those brilliant minds devised strategies for investing in bonds and derivatives using tremendous amounts of leverage, which, if things went their way, would earn outrageous returns on their partners' invested capital. The problem with the strategy was that the potential for losses was catastrophic.

Meriwether thought that the company could protect itself by using a trading strategy that employed bond spreads. It would measure the historical spread between very similar bonds—such as the yield spread between two-year Treasury bonds trading in January and March. If the spread between January and March Treasuries greatly decreased or increased in relation to its historical average, LTCM would buy one and sell the other, betting that at some time in the future the spread would close back up—which it always did because they were essentially the same bond.

LTCM often made 1% or less on a trade. That might not seem like much, but multiply 1% by the $124 billion in capital it was working with, and it amounts to a profit of $1.24 billion. Do that a couple of times a year, and you start showing outrageous returns on investors' equity investments of $4.7 billion. In the second year of operation Meriwether earned his investors a 43% return on their invested capital in LTCM, and 41% the next year.

Everything was going well until Russia surprised the world in 1998 by defaulting on its domestic debt, devaluing the ruble and declaring a moratorium on payment to foreign creditors all in the same week. That caused the bond market to panic, and LTCM's spreads all went in the wrong direction, causing the company to show a massive loss. When that happened, the banks that had loaned LTCM a total of $120 billion wanted either (1) more collateral or (2) their money back, neither of which was forthcoming. Literally overnight, LTCM became insolvent. The Federal Reserve Bank of New York went in and organized a group of Wall Street banks to take control of LTCM, and its investors lost the majority of their money.

Charlie's lesson here is that a combination of supersmart people and large amounts of leverage often ends in disaster. I might add that the combination of really dumb people and large amounts of leverage usually ends in disaster as well.

INVESTMENT MANAGERS

—

"I know one guy, he's extremely smart and a very capable investor. I asked him, 'What returns do you tell your institutional clients you will earn for them?' He said, '20%.' I couldn't believe it, because he knows that's impossible. But he said, 'Charlie, if I gave them a lower number, they wouldn't give me any money to invest!' "

—

Charlie believes that the fee-driven investment management business is insane because, as he says, "Everyone wants to be an investment manager, raise the maximum amount of money, trade like mad with one another, and then just scrape the fees off the top." Why are they so reckless with our money? Because it is not their money! Let's say I manage a hedge fund; you give me your money to invest, and I use it to help me borrow more money. I then use your money and the borrowed money to place a really big bet. If it works out, you make a ton of money and I make a ton of money in fees. It's a win-win. But if I lose it, you and the bank will be crying, not me. That, for a hedge fund, is a great business model. But first it needs to get your money. The second thing it needs to do is keep its hands on your money—it doesn't want you pulling it out and going somewhere else. So how does it do that?

INVESTMENT MANAGERS

There are two hedge fund rules for raising and keeping money. The first rule: Promise investors the sky, because if the hedge fund doesn't promise to make you a lot of money, you won't invest your money. The second rule: Any hedge fund that invests your money conservatively won't keep it for very long because the guys down the street who leveraged up, threw the dice, and won will show much higher returns. That means that in a year or two your greed will motivate you to leave my underperforming conservative fund for the winning, highly leveraged gambler down the street. So there is no economic advantage for hedge funds to be conservative with your money. Yes, they might lose a lot of your money after a few years, but when they do, you will just go find the next high flyer and the fund manager who lost your money will just go and start another fund. Don't believe me? Consider this: After the famed Wall Street bond trader John Meriwether crashed Long-Term Capital Management in 1998, he started another fund, JWM Partners, in 1999, which he successfully ran for eight years, getting assets up to $3 billion. Then the financial crisis of 2007–09 cost him 44% of the fund's assets and he had to close it. He then went on to start another fund, JM Advisors, in 2010.

The economic reality of the hedge fund business model makes it madness for hedge funds to do anything but leverage up and throw the dice. Which is, of course, why they all do it. But despair not, for the folly that these dice rollers get themselves into presents the likes of Charlie with many wonderful investment opportunities.

WAITING

—

"It's waiting that helps you as an investor, and a lot of people just can't stand to wait."

—

Blaise Pascal, the seventeenth-century French mathematician, said, "All of humanity's problems stem from man's inability to sit quietly in a room alone." Charlie agrees. You have to wait for the right company—one with a durable competitive advantage—that is selling at the right price. And when Charlie says wait, he means wait as long as it takes, which can mean years. Warren got out of the stock market in the late 1960s, and he waited five years before he found anything he was interested in buying. In the late 1990s, during the Internet bubble, Charlie and Warren gave up on finding anything to buy in the stock market, and it wasn't until 2003 that they started to find stocks attractive again. But waiting, for most investors, is not an easy thing to do. This also applies to mutual and hedge fund managers; they are driven to produce quarterly results, so waiting several years to find something good to buy is out of the question.

There is more than just waiting to find something to buy. Once you buy a stock, you have to wait for the business's underlying economics to grow the company and lift its stock price. When Charlie and Warren say that they intend to hold an investment forever, they mean forever! Who on Wall Street would ever make such a statement? That's one of the reasons Charlie and Warren have never worried about anyone mimicking their investment style—because no other institution or individual has the discipline or patience to wait as long as they can.

TAX SHELTERS

—

"In terms of business mistakes that I've seen over a long lifetime, I would say that trying to minimize taxes too much is one of the great standard causes of really dumb mistakes. . . . Anytime somebody offers you a tax shelter from here on in life, my advice would be don't buy it."

—

Charlie has seen incredible mistakes in investment judgment because some people are more concerned with not paying taxes than they are with making money. They invest in tax shelters that may be great at avoiding taxes but in reality are terrible business ventures, many of which end up losing more money than they saved their owners in taxes. Charlie and Warren have engineered their investment in Berkshire Hathaway so that it is a kind of legal tax shelter. They have accomplished this by having the company never pay a dividend, thus avoiding the tax on the dividend payment, and by holding their Berkshire stock for fifty years. That has allowed the earnings to pile up inside Berkshire. And they used the accumulated profits to build the company by acquiring other companies. The only time they have to pay the tax on their Berkshire holdings is when they sell their stock.

TAX SHELTERS

In Warren's case, since all his money is going to a charitable foundation, he will never have to pay a dime of tax on it. Why would Charlie or Warren ever buy a tax shelter when they have Berkshire Hathaway, the ultimate vehicle for avoiding or deferring the payment of taxes?

ENDURING PROBLEMS

—

"An isolated example that's very rare is much easier to endure than a perfect sea of misery that never ceases."

—

Charlie is talking about the difference between an excellent company, which might confront a major problem a few times in a span of twenty years, compared with a mediocre company, which might go from problem to problem, year after year. A perfect example of an "excellent company" is the Coca-Cola Company. Over the last fifty years Coca-Cola has screwed up twice—once when it got into the movie business and again when it reformulated its flagship product and came out with New Coke. It solved both problems by getting rid of them. The perfect example of a mediocre business that goes from one problem to another is any airline—which has union problems and fuel cost problems and is in a price-competitive business.

This bit of wisdom is also applicable to our personal lives; it is far easier to endure a brief moment of intense pain than it is to suffer a misery that drags on year after year.

SURPRISES

—

"Favorable surprises are easy to handle. It's the unfavorable surprises that cause the trouble."

—

Prepare for the worst, and hope for the best. It is always wise to be prepared for the worst. Benjamin Graham's "margin of safety" was devised to protect us from the worst. When it comes to stocks, Charlie thinks of the margin of safety in terms of price and quality—the lower the price, the higher the margin of safety; the higher the quality of the business, the higher the margin of safety. Raise the price, and the margin of safety starts to evaporate. Lower the quality of the business, and the margin of safety drops. If we buy a high-quality business at the right price, the margin of safety will protect us against long-term losses, and later on the high quality of the business will bring us many profitable surprises as the business continues to grow either internally or through acquisitions.

UNDERSTANDING THE ODDS

—

"Move only when you have the advantage—you have to understand the odds and have the discipline to bet only when the odds are in your favor."

—

Here is where it gets counterintuitive. To understand this piece of advice, you need a little bit of "Charlie history." In the late 1960s both Charlie and Warren had their own hedge fund. As the bull market of the late '60s raged on, everything became overpriced, and Warren, who was still following a Graham approach of buying bargains, could no longer find anything cheap to buy. So rather than alter his investment strategy, Warren shut down his hedge fund and returned the money to his partners, putting the vast majority of his own money into cash equivalents such as US treasuries.

Charlie kept on investing, and enjoyed great returns until the stock market crash of 1973–74, when he lost nearly half of his partners' money. He called it the worst time in his life. Warren, who was sitting on a huge amount of cash because everything running up to the crash had been overpriced, suddenly found himself surrounded by dozens of wonderful companies selling at bargain prices. Because Warren was awash in cash, he could buy them. Because Charlie didn't have any cash, he couldn't buy them. When the stock market recovered,

UNDERSTANDING THE ODDS

Charlie's investments recovered and he regained his partners' losses. But the experience so shattered him that he shut down his fund.

What did Charlie learn from all that? He learned that as stock prices rise, the odds start going against investors. And when prices fall, the odds start turning in investors' favor. He also learned that if he stays fully invested in the market as it rises, he won't have any cash to invest with when the market crashes. It doesn't matter how good the odds are; if you don't have any cash to bet with, you are never going to make a dime.

A FEW GOOD COMPANIES

—

"If you buy something because it's undervalued, then you have to think about selling it when it approaches your calculation of its intrinsic value. That's hard. But, if you can buy a few great companies, then you can sit on your ass. That's a good thing."

—

We touched on this point earlier, but it is so important that we will go over it again.

The old Benjamin Graham method of buying undervalued stocks required an investor to set a valuation on a company and then, when the company reaches that valuation, sell it. This approach fails because it requires us to sell not only mediocre companies as they approach their valuation but also great businesses that have a durable competitive advantage, thus killing all opportunity to profit from the expansion of the underlying value of a business that occurs over time.

Charlie and Warren's theory is that a company with a durable competitive advantage has business economics that will expand the underlying value of the business over time, and the more time passes, the more the company's value will expand. Thus, once the purchase is made, it is wisest to sit on the investment as long as possible, because the longer we own the company, the more it grows in value, and the more it grows in value, the richer we become.

This can best be seen with Berkshire Hathaway, which over the last fifty years has traded anywhere from below book value in the early 1970s to almost twice book value in the late 1990s. If we had bought in at below book value and sold it at twice book value, we would have made great money, but we would have missed the giant moves Berkshire made in the period from 2000 to 2016, when it more than tripled in value. If we pick the right company, as Charlie says, sitting on our ass can really pay off.

OWNERSHIP OF A BUSINESS

–

"View a stock as an ownership of the business and judge the staying quality of the business in terms of its competitive advantage."

–

Benjamin Graham, the dean of value investing, looked at owning a stock as owning part of a business. If we look at investing from the standpoint of buying a fractional interest in a business, we can make a determination of whether we are getting a bargain or paying too much. Charlie begins by figuring out what an entire company is selling for, by multiplying the share price by the number of shares outstanding. For example, a $6-per-share stock multiplied by 1 million shares outstanding equates to a market value for the whole company of $6 million. Then he asks himself what the company is worth as an economic entity from a long-term perspective. If the company is worth a lot more than its market valuation, it is a potential buy. If it is worth less, he gives it a pass, but if it has a "durable competitive advantage," he will keep an eye on it in the hope that at some future date it will be selling at a bargain price or even a fair price.

Finding a business with a durable competitive advantage means determining whether it has staying power. If we are going to buy and hold a company for twenty years, we don't want the product it is selling to become obsolete in year five. A great number of Berkshire's investments have been in companies that have manufactured the same product or provided the same service for fifty or more years. In fact, most of the wonderful businesses that Charlie and Warren own—such as the Coca-Cola Company, Wells Fargo Bank, American Express, Swiss Re, Wrigley's Gum, Kraft Foods, and even Anheuser Busch before it was bought out—have been selling the same product or service for more than a hundred years! When it comes to the truly great businesses, time is almost always on the investor's side.

RECOGNIZING REALITY

—

"I think that one should recognize reality even when one doesn't like it; indeed, especially when one doesn't like it."

—

The reality that Charlie is talking about here is when a much-loved investment enters a new realm of economic reality—which means that over time the underlying economics of the company have changed so much that the once great business is no longer such a wonderful enterprise. For Berkshire this happens periodically with its reinsurance businesses. Overcapacity in the reinsurance business means that there is too much money chasing too little business. This results in lower pricing, which means that Berkshire makes less money for reinsuring the risk. Most reinsurance companies don't accept this reality and just keep selling reinsurance policies—even when it means they will make very little money off them. Berkshire, on the other hand, just flat out stops selling reinsurance, and will wait till prices rise again before getting back into the game. As a result Berkshire has become one of the largest and most profitable reinsurance operations in the world today.

33

NOT BEING STUPID

–

"It is remarkable how much long-term advantage people like us have gotten by trying to be consistently not stupid, instead of trying to be very intelligent. There must be some wisdom in the folk saying: 'It's the strong swimmers who drown.'"

–

Strong swimmers are the ones who swim way out and potentially get themselves in trouble. Weaker swimmers stay close to shore, where it is safe. In the investing game it is the high IQ math/quant types who use the supercomplicated trading models who get themselves into trouble. Charlie isn't interested in complex mathematical models and trading strategies that Wall Street PhDs use to exploit the short-term fluctuations of the stock market. Just the opposite: he is interested in a simple investment strategy that allows him to post superior results over the long term, the foundation of which is trying not to do anything stupid. To Charlie, being stupid means spending more for a business than you get in value.

OPPORTUNITY

—

"You do get an occasional opportunity to get into a wonderful business that's being run by a wonderful manager. And, of course, that's hog heaven day."

—

Charlie believes that if you aren't buying like crazy when you have the opportunity to buy a business that has a huge potential, it is a big mistake. The key here is to buy aggressively when we have the opportunity. The problem is that to do so, one is usually buying into a tanking stock market and for most people that is a very difficult thing to do. Why? Because they see other investors losing money and it frightens them, so they become timid. The opportunity is right in front of them, but they are too scared to invest.

Also, people might not have cash at the right time to make a buy. Most investment funds are fully invested; they aren't sitting on any cash, the reason being that if the market goes up and they aren't fully invested, the cash component will pull down their rate of return, which will cause clients to leave them.

So the market tanks, the fund manager panics, and even if he did want to buy, he doesn't have the cash to do it. Everyone else is on the same sinking ship, so the fund manager looks no worse than the rest of the crowd. Everyone except Charlie and Warren, who have figured out that the ship isn't really going to sink and now is the time to buy.

THE FUTURE OF
BERKSHIRE HATHAWAY

—

*"When I came out to California, there was this playboy
and he spent all his time drinking heavily and chasing
movie stars. His banker called him in and said that he
was very nervous about his behavior. He told his banker,
'Let me tell you something: my municipal bonds don't
drink.'"*

—

Charlie is using this story to remind us that Berkshire Hathaway owns
a collection of exceptional businesses, hand selected by Charlie and
Warren because of their superior underlying economics and run by
brilliant managers. They will keep on earning Berkshire good money
long after he and Warren get off the wagon and sail on to that great
bull market in the sky.

FINANCIAL DEMENTIA

—

"There is more dementia about finance than there is about sex."

—

Very true; the financial disasters of today are almost completely forgotten in a year or two. This is probably due to the fact that in the investment business money is made by banking on the future, not lamenting the past. Because of this, most financial institutions are doomed to repeat the follies of yesteryear.

Charlie understands this and uses a company's stock price as way to position himself in late bull markets with large cash reserves in anticipation of the coming implosion and the buying opportunities it will present. He doesn't have to predict when the implosion will happen; he just has to be prepared to wait several years for stock prices to fall. The pricing component stops him from buying stocks as prices get higher and higher, which means that cash starts to build up at Berkshire. He has given up profiting from the final stages of a bull market in order to be able to position himself to buy big when the bust does come. The giant investment funds can't do that; if they miss out on the profits in the latter stages of a bull market, their clients will take their money elsewhere.

I remember sitting at the Berkshire Hathaway 1998 Annual

Meeting listening to shareholder after shareholder question why Charlie and Warren weren't investing in anything—everything was going up—and they just sat there saying over and over again that stock prices were too high. And when the bust occurred in 2000, and everyone was running for cover, they were in a position to buy and buy big. They did the exact same thing in 2008. How do we know when the stock market is too high? When the financial press starts writing articles about how Charlie and Warren have lost their Midas touch.

BUSINESS VALUATIONS

–

"If people weren't wrong so often, we wouldn't be so rich."

–

Investors are often wrong about business valuations; most of the time they think a company is worth far more than it will ever earn. But that doesn't help us; what helps us is when they do just the opposite, when they think that a business is worth far less than its long-term economics indicate and therefore misprice it on the downside. It's the mispricing on the downside that gives Charlie his buying opportunities. And that is something the investing herd manages to do in a big way about once every eight to ten years.

If you want to look at where the market was grossly wrong in its valuations and Charlie and Warren took advantage of the situation, look at the major recessions and stock market crashes over the last fifty-five years. There was the Kennedy stock market slide of 1962, which gave Warren his buying opportunity in Berkshire Hathaway. There was the 1973–74 stock market crash, which gave Warren his buying opportunity in the *Washington Post*. When Federal Reserve Chairman Paul Volcker raised interest rates to 14% in 1978–80, killing the stock market, Berkshire was busy buying General Foods, R. J. Reynolds, and the Times Mirror Company. The stock market crash in October 1987 gave Berkshire the opportunity to start buying

Coke stock, which it continued buying well into 1988. The banking recession of 1990 gave Berkshire its opportunity to start buying Wells Fargo. In the late 1990s the Internet bubble caused stock prices to soar, but nobody wanted the old-school brick-and-mortar businesses. Berkshire bought Star Furniture, Dairy Queen, General Re, and NetJets. When the Internet bubble burst and 9/11 beat the stock market down in 2001, Berkshire bought its positions in H&R Block and Moody's Corporation. The subprime blowup in 2007–09 and the ensuing stock market crash set the stage for Berkshire to acquire the preferred equity or debt of GE, Harley-Davidson, Bank of America, and Goldman Sachs; and in 2010, as the stock market started to recover, Berkshire acquired stock in Burlington Northern Railroad, whose share price had been beaten down in the 2007–09 crash. Why were all the other investors wrong? They were short-sighted and panicked, whereas Charlie and Warren were playing the long-term game and knew exactly what they were looking for.

WAITING IS THE HARDEST PART

—

"You have to be very patient, you have to wait until something comes along, which, at the price you're paying, is easy. That's contrary to human nature, just to sit there all day long doing nothing, waiting. It's easy for us, we have a lot of other things to do. But for an ordinary person, can you imagine just sitting for five years doing nothing? You don't feel active, you don't feel useful, so you do something stupid."

—

We've talked about Charlie's view of patience earlier on. But just in case there are any doubting Thomases among you, I wanted you to read Charlie's statement on the subject at the 2014 Daily Journal Annual Meeting. This important statement helps explain one of the last great mysteries of Charlie's equation for creating fantastic wealth. And believe me when I tell you that out of the forty thousand people who attend the Berkshire Hathaway annual meeting, which includes thousands of investment professionals, there might be ten people there who actually understand this piece of advice and are able to put it into practice. So I want to walk through it line by line—to explore all of its nuances. Because if you get anything out of this book, you will learn the importance that Charlie puts on patience.

Most investors are impatient. Because of this they fail right out of the gate. Why? Because stocks are almost always selling at prices that are way above their long-term intrinsic value. It is the nature of the beast. If you wake up one morning determined to invest your money, your chances of finding an investment that would meet Charlie's standards is almost zero. So you settle for something less, when you could have gotten something more if you had just waited. Which Charlie says is easy to do because you don't have to pay anyone to wait.

Charlie's approach is contrary to human nature, but right there it should tell you that it is a winning investment strategy. For one of the most successful of all investment strategies is to be a contrarian investor—to go in the opposite direction—to buy when others are selling. And not being in a hurry is contrary to everyone who is in a hurry, which is just about everyone else in the world.

Think of it this way: Charlie isn't out looking for an investment, he is waiting for the right long-term investment—at the right price—to come to him. Yes, he keeps his eyes wide open to make sure he sees it when it arrives, which is why he reads a lot, to make sure he sees it when it shows up. But if it doesn't show up, he just keeps on reading. Is that hard to do? Imagine that you go see an investment adviser and he tells you it might take five years to find the right investment. Most people would stand up and leave and go find another investment adviser. It truly is not in people's nature to wait, which is the advantage Charlie has over all of us.

Because most people are in a rush, because they can't be like

Charlie and wait five years for the right long-term investment—at the right price—to show up, and since most of the time stocks sell at prices in excess of their intrinsic value, most investors end up overpaying for the stocks they are buying. So my question to you is this: Are you one of the 99% of investors who are in a rush and end up overpaying for your investments? Or are you part of Charlie's 1% club who have the patience to wait five years, if necessary, to find the right long-term investment selling at the right price?

WADING IN

–

"We have a history when things are really horrible of wading in when no one else will."

–

As we have said repeatedly throughout this book, the only way that Charlie can do that is if he is sitting on a pile of cash in waiting to take advantage of some financial calamity. The reason that other investors don't step in is that they don't have the cash to buy anything with. Most investment funds are 100% invested in the market. Why are they 100% invested? Because cash offers a low return and having a lot of cash can severely hurt a fund's performance.

Also, there are funds that borrow money, meaning they are more than 100% invested. They borrow money to increase the return on investors' capital, which also generates larger fees for the fund manager. So when the market goes down, fully invested funds lose money—lots of money—especially leveraged funds. In a market crash, open-ended funds, where investors are putting in money and pulling it out on a daily basis, not only see their portfolios shrink in value but also have investors yanking money out of the fund to the tune of hundreds of millions.

WADING IN

The bottom line is that in a bear market such institutions—mutual funds, hedge funds, and the like—are in no position to buy anything. Which leaves all the low-hanging fruit for the likes of Charlie and Warren.

ACADEMIC SORCERY

—

*"By and large I don't think too much of finance professors.
It is a field with witchcraft."*

—

The big problem with finance professors—besides being addicted to the mediocrity of diversification—is that they preach the efficient market theory. Basically this theory says that the market is efficient, so no one can beat it and we are all doomed to average results. What the finance professors completely miss is that from a long-term perspective individual companies have moments of inefficiency when the shortsighted "efficient" stock market misprices them relative to their underlying long-term economics. The finance professors, having never studied population biology as Charlie has, have a difficult time understanding that multiple strategies of exploitation can interact with one another to the point that efficiency in one can create an inefficiency in another.

Let me give you an example: The stock market panics, as doom and gloom loom on the horizon, the vast majority of investors flee, seeking the safety of cash, driving stock prices downward. From a shortsighted perspective the market is being efficient in its reaction to the information at hand. Where "inefficiency" can appear is when investors rush for the exit, driving stock prices downward, which can cause a mispricing on the downside relative to a company's long-term economic value. Why does the market misprice stocks? Either it doesn't care about the long-term value of businesses in its moment of panic and/or it simply can't see their long-term economic value. Which is what happened to Coca-Cola and Wells Fargo when Charlie and Warren were buying them.

Over the years Charlie and Warren have refined their strategy to include holding large reserves of ready cash and targeting only companies that have a durable competitive advantage. But their long-term strategy of exploitation is wholly dependent on the short-sighted stock market acting in an efficient manner and creating brief moments of inefficiency from a long-term perspective. That is how Charlie beats the law of averages and proves the finance professors and their financial incantations wrong.

GREEDY BANKERS

–

"Mortgage lending became a dirty way to make money. You take people that can't handle credit and try to make very high returns by abusing and encouraging their stupidity—that's not the way I want to make money in banking. You should try to make money by selling people things that are good for the customer."

–

In the old days banks kept home mortgages on their own books, so they were very careful whom they loaned money to. But then the business model changed and banks started selling the mortgages they wrote to other companies. It no longer mattered whom they loaned money to, because they were going to sell off the mortgage as soon as they wrote it. The game then became the more home mortgages the bank wrote, the more money the bank made. And if a homeowner defaulted, who cared? The bank was out of the equation. That's how banking went from being a boring business with boring salaries, to being an exciting business with outrageous salaries.

INVESTING IN BANKS

—

"I don't think anyone should buy a bank if they don't have a feel for the bankers. Banking is a business that is a very dangerous place for an investor. Without deep insight, stay away."

—

One of the hallmarks of Charlie and Warren's investments in banks is that they always praise the management of the banks they invest in. What they praise is management's being obsessed with operating efficiency—it keeps costs low—and risk management—it avoids taking large derivative positions and writing shaky mortgages. Be it Wells Fargo or U.S. Bank or Bank of America, it is all about the quality and integrity of the management.

And why management? Because the quality of management is something tangible that Charlie and Warren can get their heads around, whereas a bank's financial statements are often so convoluted that not even the best financial analysts can understand them.

NO SINGLE FORMULA

–

*"There isn't a single formula. You need to know a lot
about business and human nature and the numbers. . . .
It is unreasonable to expect that there is a magic system
that will do it for you."*

–

People are looking for a simple method they can learn from reading
one book that will make them rich. It doesn't happen that way—
unless they get real lucky. One is actually better off reading a hundred
business biographies than a hundred books on investing. Why?
Because if we learn the history of a hundred different business models,
we learn when the businesses had tough times and how they got
through them; we also learn what made them great, or not so great.
Which allows us to get a feel for whether or not a business has some
kind of durable competitive advantage working in its favor, which
is key in figuring out if it would make a great long-term investment.

Just reading books on business isn't enough; one should also
add in a couple of semesters of accounting (which is the language of
business), a couple of semesters of economics, and a good course on
central banking so one understands the power of the Federal Reserve
Bank to come to the market's rescue (most MBA courses are sorely
lacking in this). Then one will be in a good position to start looking

for a winning investment. But then the search for a good investment takes even more reading—so count on reading two or three hundred annual reports a year and the *Wall Street Journal* every day.

Now do you understand why most people are looking for a simple, easy system for them to use. The funny part of this equation is that they are the ones who often do stupid things in the stock market that people in the know—like Charlie—end up profiting from. As Warren says, if you get into a card game and you can't figure out who is the patsy, then you're the patsy.

ON TECHNOLOGY

–

"The great lesson in microeconomics is to discriminate between when technology is going to help you and when it's going to kill you."

–

New technology can either damage an existing business or increase its profitability.

The first question we should ask is: Will the new technology be a threat to the existing business model? Cars replaced buggies and horses. The telephone replaced the telegraph. Computers and printers replaced the typewriter.

The next question is: Will the new technology enhance the business? Here the question gets a bit more complicated. Whether or not a company will benefit from a change in technology is dependent on the type of business it is.

If you're a commodity-type business, which sells a product or service that a number of other companies also supply, any technology breakthrough that will lower costs and improve margins will probably also be picked up by your competitors—which means you will lose any competitive edge the technology provides. But worse than that is when one of your competitors uses the cost savings the new technology provides to cut prices and increase its market share.

As an example: New technology XY will deliver a 10% cost savings to our firm—which is a good thing. Our competitor also buys New Technology XY and achieves a 10% cost savings. Now both companies are ahead; both are saving 10%. But if our competitor wakes up one morning and decides to use that 10% cost savings to cut prices by 10% to add to his market share, we are going to have to also cut our prices by 10% or we are going to lose market share. So at the end of the day, in a commodity-type business with lots of competitors, it is only the customer who profits from the new technology.

When a company has a durable competitive advantage in a particular market niche, there are no competitors. With such businesses the 10% cost savings that the new technology provides is not eroded by price-cutting by competitors seeking to take market share. As an example: If Coke develops a new technology that can reduce its production costs by 10 cents a bottle, it can bring that savings down to its bottom line, because even if Pepsi develops the same technology and cuts the price of its product, history has shown people will still buy the slightly more expensive Coke because Coke owns a piece of the consumers' mind and has their trust and buyer loyalty. The ability of a company with a durable competitive advantage to utilize a new technology to actually cut costs and increase its profit margins is one of the advantages that it has over the commodity-type business.

SUCCESSFUL INVESTING

—

"Successful investing requires this crazy combination of gumption and patience, and then being ready to pounce when the opportunity presents itself, because in this world opportunities just don't last very long."

—

In March 2009, in the middle of the great crash (when everyone thought the US government was going to have to nationalize all the big US banks), Charlie bought for his company, Daily Journal, 1.6 million shares of Wells Fargo Bank, at an average cost he estimates at $8.58 per share. Today Wells Fargo's stock trades at around $47 a share. He was able to do so because (1) he was focused on looking for a good investment, and (2) he was sitting on a pile of cash, patiently waiting until an opportunity presented itself. And last but not least, he understood Wells Fargo well enough that he knew that there was little chance of the bank ever becoming insolvent or the government taking it over. That buying opportunity lasted but a couple of weeks, and when it was available, Charlie had the gumption to pounce on it.

BEATING THE AVERAGE

–

"It is in the nature of stock markets that they go down. So people suffer then. Conservative investing and steady saving without expecting miracles is the way to go. Some people in this room can figure out how to average twice the rate of return. I can't teach everyone else to do it. It is pretty difficult."

–

It is difficult but not impossible to do better than the stock market average. But it takes a lot of reading to get there. For most people it is easier and safer if they just save their money, buy into an index fund anytime there is a bear market, and then just hold it forever. Then when they retire, they can sell it off as needed. But for those who want to invest time and energy in study, the stock market is a sea of endless opportunity that can produce unimaginable wealth.

COMMISSIONS

—

"Everywhere there is a large commission, there is a high probability of a rip-off."

—

Commission equals incentives. In Charlie's world incentives drive motivation on both the conscious and subconscious levels. Financial planners and stockbrokers working on commission are motivated to take us out of one investment and put us into another investment because they make money in doing so. The more activity in our account, the more money they make. So they find reasons for buying and selling on our accounts, and most of the time they are the ones getting rich, while we are the ones who are getting poor. Or as the comedian Woody Allen once said, "A stockbroker is someone who invests other people's money until it's all gone."

PART II

–

CHARLIE ON BUSINESS, BANKING, AND THE ECONOMY

THE GREAT DEPRESSION

–

"You don't ever want to do anything to push an economy to collapse. Terrible things result."

–

The Great Depression of the 1930s, which Charlie lived through, is now, for most Americans, but a distant memory and a couple of pages in a history book. Forgotten are the millions of people out of work all over the world and the devastating impact that took many nations decades to fully recover from. Just how bad was it? Consider this: During the Great Recession of 2007–09, worldwide GDP fell 1%; during the Great Depression, worldwide GDP fell by 15%. During the Great Depression, the United States experienced a 50% drop in foreign trade and a 60% drop in crop prices, and unemployment rose to a high of 25%. The European economies were decimated to the point that it caused entire nations to lose faith in their democratic institutions, which gave birth to the rise of fascism in a desperate attempt to fix the seemingly unfixable. The end result was a world war that caused Europe and the rest of the world to suffer unimaginable horrors of death and destruction. Charlie lived through that age and knows all too well that a nation's descent into hell begins with the collapsing of its economy. That if a democracy can't find the strength to control its financial institutions, eventually the people will empower a despot who will.

REGULATING BANKS

–

"Banks will not rein themselves in voluntarily. They need adult supervision."

–

Charlie has always seen the deregulation of the banking industry as pure folly on the part of Congress. He saw the ushering in of the Glass-Steagall Act of 1933, which separated speculative investment banks from conservative commercial banks, as the beginning of a period of great prosperity in America. He thought the repealing of Glass-Steagall in 1999 was an invitation to banking folly because it allowed commercial banks to function as investment banks and speculate with depositors' money. The 2007–09 collapse of Wall Street proved to the world that Charlie was right: repealing Glass-Steagall was one of the dumbest things Congress has ever done.

TOO BIG TO FAIL

–

"Capitalism without failure is like religion without hell."

–

When the Federal Reserve chairman, Ben Bernanke, and the head of the US Treasury, Hank Paulson, decided that Goldman Sachs, Citicorp, Merrill Lynch, and AIG were too big to fail, they were telling the world that the government wouldn't let those financial institutions go under. If a Wall Street bank has no fear of going bankrupt, its managers have no fear when it comes to leveraging their businesses and gambling with their depositors' and shareholders' money. By creating a government-financed safety net for those institutions, the Fed set the stage for another cycle of financial institution folly and destruction. But such a dark cloud can have a silver lining, because as it creates great upheaval in the stock market, there will be moments when investors rush for the door, and in those moments of panic, stocks of wonderful businesses will sell for bargain prices in relation to their underlying long-term economics. As we said earlier, the 2007–09 bank failures created a buying opportunity in Wells Fargo Bank, which Charlie jumped on. One man's idea of hell can be another man's idea of paradise, especially if it means cheap stock prices on great businesses.

BORROWED MONEY

–

"We have monetized houses in this country in a way that's never occurred before. Ask Joe how he bought a new Cadillac—from borrowing on his house. . . . We have financial institutions, including those with big names, extending high-cost credit to the least able people. I find a lot of it revolting. Just because it's a free market doesn't mean it's honorable."

–

I guess this means that Charlie is not in the "let the buyer beware" club. But we live in a country whose Federal Reserve Bank has taken it upon itself to rid us of unemployment. Part of its strategy for doing this has been to make consumers feel rich so they spend more money, which should stimulate the economy and in the process create more jobs. The easiest way for the Fed to put more money into the hands of American consumers is to make it easy for consumers to borrow money on credit cards and the equity in their homes. The Fed encourages borrowing by lowering interest rates and by turning a blind eye to banks and mortgage companies' loosening their credit requirements. The problem with all this borrowed money and consumer spending is that it creates an economic bubble; eventually the bubble bursts, and when it does, stock prices collapse, the economy tanks, people lose their jobs, and home owners can't pay back all the money they borrowed. Which creates an even bigger nightmare.

FREE-MARKET FOLLY

–

"These crazy booms should be watched. Alan Greenspan didn't think so. He's a capable man but he's an idiot. You should not make him the father of all banking. His hero is Ayn Rand. It's an unlikely place to look for wisdom. A lot of people think that if an ax murderer goes around killing people in a free market it's all right."

–

Alan Greenspan, the head of the Federal Reserve Bank from 1987 to 2006, following the free-market preaching of the Russian-born writer/philosopher Ayn Rand, completely ignored both the stock market Internet bubble in the late 1990s and the housing bubble in the early 2000s; those led to the subprime mortgage meltdown in 2007–09 that almost destroyed the world's economy. Greenspan believed that government shouldn't interfere at all with the markets, which meant not interfering with Wall Street's excesses. This seems bizarre given that anytime the stock market started to crash Greenspan aggressively used the Fed to pump money into the market and stop the decline.

Greenspan's successor, Ben Bernanke, became head of the Fed in 2006 and continued to let the housing bubble grow unabated. When it finally burst, Bernanke did what his predecessor had done:

he printed money and pumped it into the economy, not only to stop the crash but also to pull unemployment down. During his eight-year tenure the Fed printed more than $3 trillion and put it into circulation to stimulate the economy, which caused asset inflation and both the stock and housing markets to once again bubble. Or as New York Yankee Yogi Berra once said, "It's déjà vu all over again."

BANKING DEREGULATION

–

"People really thought that giving a predatory class of people the ability to do whatever they wanted was free-market enterprise. It wasn't. It was legalized armed robbery. And it was incredibly stupid."

–

If we were being kind, we would say that Charlie is basically saying that ex–Federal Reserve Chairman Alan Greenspan and ex–US Treasury head Robert Rubin, two of the major architects of the deregulation of the banking industry in the late 1990s, got it completely wrong. They were major proponents of free-market enterprise, which led to the financial meltdown in 2008 and the bankruptcy or near bankruptcy of nearly every major Wall Street investment bank. But what Charlie is really saying is that it was incredibly stupid on their part to deregulate the banks. Why? Because the management of an unregulated bank or insurance company has an incentive to leverage up—borrow more money—and make huge speculative bets. If the bets are successful, the management team gets tens of millions of dollars in bonuses, but if the bank loses the bets, it is the shareholders and depositors who are on the hook for the billions of dollars in losses. If a couple of large banks crash at the same time, it is possible to bring down an entire economy. History has repeatedly shown us that government regulation is the only thing that stops banking professionals from leveraging up and gambling with not only other people's money but our nation's economic well-being as well.

WALL STREET EXCESSES

–

"We have a higher percentage of the intelligentsia engaged in buying and selling pieces of paper and promoting trading activity than in any past era. A lot of what I see now reminds me of Sodom and Gomorrah. You get activity feeding on itself, envy and imitation. When it happened in the past, there were bad consequences."

–

Wall Street in the year 2007 resembled the kingdoms of Sodom and Gomorrah. The subprime money flowed, the bonuses were huge, the parties were wild, and McMansions and expensive sports cars were the perks of the day. But the greatest sin of all was packaging up subprime mortgages and selling them as AAA-rated paper to the unsuspecting hungry masses. In the biblical tale of old, God destroyed Sodom and Gomorrah for their wicked indiscretions. But in our story God, dressed as the Federal Reserve's Ben Bernanke and the US Treasury's Hank Paulson, stepped in to save the infidels right before they fell into the abyss. Sometimes it is better to save the sinners than it is to take down an entire nation with them. This is especially true if you happen to be one of the sinners.

THE WEALTH EFFECT

—

"The wealth effect is the extent to which consumer spending is goosed upward due to increases in stock prices. Of course it exists, but to what extent? I made a speech a while back in which I said that the wealth effect is greater than economists believe. I still say this."

—

If people believe that their house and investments are going up in value, they will be more willing to spend more, which is good for the economy. However, if they believe that their house and investments are going down in value, they will stop buying things, which is bad for the economy. This is the wealth effect.

Ex–Federal Reserve Chairman Ben Bernanke, in his quest to revive the economy and lower the unemployment rate, became enamored with this theory. He used the wealth effect to justify pumping trillions of dollars into the economy via lower interest rates and the printing of money to finance the government's deficit spending. And it worked; asset prices went up and people felt richer, so they spent more, which stimulated the economy, which caused unemployment rates to drop. That, of course, made investors the world over very, very happy.

PRINTING MONEY

–

"I think democracies are prone to inflation because politicians will naturally spend—they have the power to print money and will use money to get votes."

–

Keep those printing presses running! One of the reasons the United States will never default on its debt is that it has the power to print the dollars it needs. How does it do that? The Federal Reserve Bank prints the money and then goes into the open market and buys US government Treasury bonds or any other debt it wants to buy. Say the US Treasury needs $100 billion to pay off some US government debt coming due; it simply issues more debt, which the Federal Reserve Bank buys on the open market. As a rule the Federal Reserve Bank doesn't like doing this; it would rather the US government borrow its money from places like China—which at present owns $1.2 trillion in US government bonds (which means the US government has borrowed $1.2 trillion from China). But China doesn't have to worry about the good old USA defaulting on its debt, because the Federal Reserve Bank can always print an extra $1.2 trillion and loan it to the US government to pay off the bonds the US government sold to China.

The problem that Greece, Italy, and Spain have is that when they made the euro their currency, their respective central banks gave up the power to print money and turned that power over to the European Central Bank. So unless the ECB is willing to print an extra couple of hundred billion euros for them, Greece, Italy, and Spain all have the potential to default on their debt and cause a systemic collapse of the world's financial system.

ASSET INFLATION

—

"I remember the $0.05 hamburger and a $0.40-per-hour minimum wage, so I've seen a tremendous amount of inflation in my lifetime. Did it ruin the investment climate? I think not."

—

As a hamburger rises in price, so does the price of the shares of the company that sells the hamburger. Inflation raises the prices of both commodities and assets, and shares in a company represent ownership in the company's assets. Inflation is the friend of people who own assets. Inflation is also the enemy of the people who own cash or bonds. Why? When the Federal Reserve prints money and circulates it into the economy, interest rates go down. This drives up the prices of financial assets such as stocks and real estate. But the Fed's printing of more money also means that our dollars buy less and less, which means that things cost more and more. Fifty years ago a hamburger cost $0.40, now it costs $7; and a house that cost $50,000 in 1965 now costs $500,000; and the Dow Jones Industrial Average, which stood at 910 points in 1965, now stands at 17,000. If you hang on to cash, it will buy less and less every year. If you bought twenty-year bonds in 1996 and cashed them in 2016, the cash you got back bought less than it did when you bought the bonds.

ASSET INFLATION

Inflation really helps the banking and insurance industries. Since that $50,000 house is now a $500,000 house, people have to borrow $450,000 more from the bank. And there will be a hell of a lot more bank fees for a loan that size than for a $50,000 loan. The property insurance company is also going to earn a whole lot more on insuring a $500,000 property than it ever earned insuring our $50,000 property.

In the example above, both the bank and the insurance company saw inflation cause a 1,000% rise in business, but neither institution had to add any more employees or increase the size of its operating plant. Now you know why Charlie and Warren are so big on insurance companies and banks: not only are they the perfect hedge against inflation, they actually benefit from it. For banks and insurance companies, inflation truly is the gift that keeps on giving.

OIL RESERVES

—

"I think the hydrocarbon reserves in the United States are one of the most precious things we have, every bit as precious as the topsoil of Iowa. Just as I don't want to export all the topsoil in Iowa to Iran or someplace, just because they are willing to give us some money, I love the hydrocarbon reserves we have in the ground. The fashion is to be independent and to use them up as fast as we can. I think that's insanity as a national policy."

—

Here Charlie is talking about our nation's oil reserves. He believes they are a precious resource and should be saved because oil is so necessary to our economy and national security. Our hydrocarbon reserves are the chemical feedstock that we use to propel our autos and power our jets, and to make fertilizer, synthetic clothing, plastic, and asphalt, lubricate machinery, and generate electricity. Without oil our country would grind to a halt in an instant. Charlie thinks a national policy to become oil independent and burn up all our oil supplies as fast as we can is crazy. Because when our oil is completely gone we will be at the mercy of the countries that are still oil producers. He advocates that we should save our oil for a rainy day and burn up Saudi Arabia's oil instead.

KOREA

—

"Koreans came up from nothing in the auto business. They worked 84 hours a week with no overtime for more than a decade. At the same time every Korean child came home from grade school, and worked with a tutor for four full hours in the afternoon and the evening, driven by these Tiger Moms. Are you surprised when you lose to people like that? Only if you're a total idiot."

—

Charlie grew up during the Great Depression, in which everyone, if he could even find a job, worked tirelessly to put food on the table. But as time went on and the country became richer and richer, Americans started getting lazy. Gone is the work ethic that drove people to work ten hours a day, six days a week. Koreans, like our grandparents, are far more driven to succeed. What Charlie is saying is that in the global economy we now live in, the new winners will be the hardworking Koreas of the world, not the now fat and sassy winners of yesteryear.

CARROTS & STICKS

—

"If we're going to prosper, we have to work. We have to have people subject to carrots and sticks. If you take away the stick the whole system won't work. You can't vote yourself rich. It's an idiotic idea."

—

Charlie is a true "nose to the grindstone" capitalist at heart. Here he is saying that a nation has to work, it has to grow food, it has to build roads, buildings, and factories, and it has to make products that it can sell. If people don't work, they will be hungry and homeless; that is the stick. It wasn't greed that drove our grandparents to work so hard, it was the fear that they wouldn't be able to pay the rent and their family would go hungry. Today that fear is gone. It has been replaced with a sense of entitlement that demands that health care be free, that a college education be free, that free food and housing be provided if one is out of work. Our nation is losing its will to work, maybe not because it has grown lazy but because it has lost its fear of not working.

OUT-OF-CONTROL BANKERS

—

"I do not think you can trust bankers to control them-
selves. They are like heroin addicts."

—

Heroin addicts can destroy both an individual and his family. Bankers can destroy themselves and an entire nation's economy. Bankers are entrusted with an enormous amount of other people's money and should be conservative in investing it, but what often happens is that they use the money they have been entrusted with to leverage up—borrow more money—and then speculate with it under the guise of "investing." They do so because if they win the bet they get to pay themselves millions of dollars in salaries and bonuses, all along telling the American public not to worry about the leverage because professional risk managers have it under control (the same professional risk managers who just happen to be the ones who destroyed their Wall Street banks in the subprime mortgage meltdown of 2007–09). The only thing that can stop banks from becoming excessively leveraged is heavy regulation by the US government, which banks constantly fight to keep from happening. In 2014 alone JPMorgan Chase spent $6.2 million lobbying the US Congress. Collectively, in 2014, commercial banks spent $60 million lobbying Congress. What did they lobby against? Government regulation of the banking industry. The point that Charlie is making is that a great many bankers have become addicted to leverage and speculation; it is the lifeblood of their quest to become both rich and powerful.

DERIVATIVE DANGER

–

"If you intelligently trade derivatives it's like a license to steal, so you can understand why they all want to do it . . . but what is the big plus in having everyone gamble with everyone else? I lived in a world with low gambling for decades when I was younger and I liked it better. I think it was better for the country. It's like having thousands of professional poker players. What damn good are they doing for anybody?"

–

The problem with derivatives trading is that it is very hard for bankers to control themselves when they are easily making tons of money. They tend to get carried away with excess and in the process get themselves into serious trouble. If it is really bad, they can blow up the financial system, tank the stock market, destroy the economy, and put millions of people out of work.

According to Paul Wilmott, who holds a doctorate in applied mathematics from Oxford University, the notional value of the world's derivatives market has reached $1.2 quadrillion (which is a humongous number, equal to $1,200 trillion). This is approximately twenty times as large as the world economy, which is approximately $60 trillion. The derivatives market is now 20% larger than in 2008, the last time we had a financial crisis that involved derivatives. And what is US bank exposure to this derivative risk? Consider this: JPMorgan Chase has $2 trillion in total assets and total risk exposure to derivatives of more than $52.9 trillion; Citibank has total assets of $1.3 trillion and total risk exposure to derivatives of more than $52 trillion; Bank of America has total assets of $1.6 trillion and total risk exposure to derivatives of $26.6 trillion; Goldman Sachs has total assets of $143 billion (that's billion) and total risk exposure to derivative of $44.4 trillion (that's trillion).

If you are a bank, here is the superfun part: that $1.2 quadrillion derivatives market is mind-numbingly complex and completely unregulated, and the banks' traders rule the roost. Anytime the US government even hints that it will regulate derivatives trading, an army of bank lobbyists swarms down upon Washington, DC, and stops it by reminding our members of Congress who really owns them (and it isn't you and me). But it gets even better. Consider this: there is no one—that's right, no one—in government, in academia, or in the banks themselves who has a real grasp of all the dangers that lurk inside the largest financial bubble the world has ever seen.

CARRY-TRADE FOLLY

–

"There's a lot of leverage in those carry-trade games. Other people are more certain than I am that the aircraft can always be leased."

–

This is insightful. Charlie said this back in 2005, three full years before a carry trade blew up and destroyed Lehman Brothers and several other Wall Street firms. A carry trade is the borrowing of large amounts of money at one rate and using it to buy an asset that earns a higher rate of return. Here Charlie is talking about borrowing money and using it to buy an airplane, which can be leased for a higher amount than the loan payment. The profit is the difference between the interest costs of the loan and the lease payments. The only catch to this equation is that if the company that leases the airplane defaults on the lease, there is a loan that needs to be repaid but no lease payments to pay it with.

Where Lehman Brothers and the other investment banks screwed up is they were borrowing billions of dollars in the short-term commercial paper market and then lending it out for subprime mortgages for ten and twenty years. When Lehman's short-term paper came due, the lending institutions buying its paper would just roll the loans over. But then an unexpected thing happened: people started defaulting on their subprime mortgages, and suddenly Lehman didn't have those interest payments coming in the door, which meant that it didn't have the money to pay the interest on the loans the banks made to it. When the banks figured that out, they refused to roll the loans over, and Lehman filed for bankruptcy within a week.

CORRUPTION IN ASIA

—

"You cannot just go invest in China, however. The first movers can get killed. There's a saying in Indonesia: 'What you're calling corrupt is Asian family values.'"

—

In 2002 Charlie and Warren did finally invest in China; they bought $500 million worth of stock in the oil company PetroChina and later sold it for $3.5 billion.

After Charlie's warning about corruption, why did they trust PetroChina? The Chinese government owns 88% of it; in fact, the Chinese government controls twenty-nine of the thirty largest publicly traded companies in China. If we own shares in any one of them, we effectively have the Chinese government as a partner, and instead of bailing out shady CEOs, as the US government does, the Chinese government puts them into a cold, dark cell in which to contemplate their evil ways. Which is why Charlie and Warren could invest $500 million in a Chinese company and still get plenty of beauty sleep at night.

THE MIRACLE OF CHINA

–

"If you take what China has done from what China was, there's been no achievement on this scale in the entire history of the world."

–

Once upon a time China was a backward communist agricultural society with a Soviet-styled planned economy. It was the kind of country that would have made the famed free-market economist Milton Friedman throw up his hands in disgust. But beginning in 1979 China started down the path of transforming itself onto a dynamic market-oriented industrial/high-tech economy that embraced the tenets of capitalism with a communist twist. In just thirty short years China has become the world's second largest economy. It is the world's largest consumer and producer of textiles, cameras, cell phones, and computers and the largest producer of steel and automobiles.

In 2008 Berkshire Hathaway invested $230 million in BYD Company, a Chinese version of the United States' Tesla Motors. BYD is the largest Chinese manufacturer of autos in China and a major manufacturer of rechargeable batteries. Charlie has called its founder and CEO, Wang Chuanfu, a combination of Thomas Edison and General Electric CEO Jack Welch. Who knew the Chinese would turn out to be so good at being capitalists?

FREE TRADE

–

"I don't see how we bring back that age where an uneducated man can march ahead rapidly. As long as we have free trade and worldwide competition, and I don't want to stop having free trade with a big nuclear power like China. China and the United States have to get along. Each country would be out of its mind not to get along with the other. I think trade helps us to get along."

–

The shifting of American factory jobs to China pretty much ended the period in US economic history in which an uneducated man or woman could go to work on a factory floor and get ahead. Why? The first reason is that good manufacturing jobs for the uneducated are simply no longer here; they are in places such as China and Mexico. The second is that good jobs in the United States require education and training.

As far as free trade helping US-Chinese relations, it actually has more to do with the fact that China owns approximately $1.2 trillion in US government notes and bonds—which means that it has loaned the US government approximately $1.2 trillion. If someone owes you $1.2 trillion and you want to be paid back, you get up every morning wishing them the best of economic health. It's not free trade that helps the United States get along with the Chinese, it's the $1.2 trillion the Chinese want to be paid back; and for the United States it is the other $1 trillion in new debt it needs to sell to finance the government's ever-increasing deficit spending. Add in concerns about nuclear weapons, and Charlie is right: the two countries are out of their minds if they don't get along with each other.

THE MISER

–

"I don't care if somebody makes a lot of money and holds it like a miser. Most people have a vast propensity to spend, helped by spouses and children."

–

One of the greatest misconceptions in life is that the rich squirrel their gold away in some deep, dark vault, where it does no one any good. That may have been true two hundred years ago. However, in the modern age the rich keep their loot in banks and investment funds, which either loan it out to people and businesses in need or invest it in commercial enterprises. Banks and investment funds are distributors of capital in our communities. If they don't loan money out or invest it, they don't make any money, so there is a very strong impetus to make loans and find businesses to invest in. This is good for the economy, which is good for everyone. However, if there weren't any rich people, there would be little surplus capital in the banks and investment funds to finance things such as buying a home, constructing an office building, financing the development of new industry, making loans to local governments, and the like. The top 1% controls 39% of the world's wealth, but what that really means is that 39% of the world's wealth is tucked away in the world's banks and investment funds, which are very busy investing this surplus wealth in the world's economy. Which is a very good thing for the other 99% of the world.

CORPORATE TAXES

—

"If I were running the world I would have low corporate taxes, and get at the yearning for equality some other way, like consumption taxes."

—

In the free trade of the world today, corporations can move freely from one country to another. A high corporate tax rate in one country will drive a corporation out of that country into another that has a lower tax rate. And the corporations that migrate to lower-tax venues, when they get there, will put their surplus capital into local banks. Want to know how Singapore and Hong Kong became the two financial centers of Asia? Low corporate taxes attracted rich corporations to them and with the rich corporations came their surplus capital, which was tucked away in local banks such as the OCBC Bank in Singapore and the Bank of China in Hong Kong, where it has been used to help finance the economic miracles of Singapore and Hong Kong. Charlie is in favor of using lower tax rates as a means to attract and keep more corporations in the United States.

REDUCING STANDARDS

–

"The whole world is better when you don't reduce engineering standards in finance. We skipped a total disaster by a hair's breadth. . . . I'm a big fan of the people who took us through the crisis. I'm not a big fan of the people who caused the crisis. Some of them deserve to be in the lowest circle of hell."

–

Charlie is talking about the near-collapse of our financial system in 2008. When a bridge is built, engineering standards require it to be able to support tons more weight than is expected ever to be on the bridge. This creates a margin of safety for the bridge that ensures that it will never collapse. In the banking world the margin of safety is measured by a bank's debt-to-equity ratio. The lower the ratio, the less likely the bank will fail in a recession. The higher the ratio, the more likely the bank will fail in a recession. Engineering standards in banking would dictate that banks keep very low debt-to-equity ratios to ensure that they can withstand any disruptions in the financial markets. In 2007 the investment banks of Wall Street did just the opposite and drove their debt-to-equity ratios to all-time highs. Some banks had $38 of debt for every $1 of equity they held on their balance sheet. When the Great Recession hit, many of them literally collapsed overnight.

PART III

–

CHARLIE'S PHILOSOPHY APPLIED TO BUSINESS AND INVESTING

BUY AND HOLD

–

"We just keep our heads down and handle the headwinds and tailwinds as best we can, and take the result after a period of years."

–

Once Charlie gets his hands on an excellent business at a fair price, he knows that the smart thing to do is to hold on to it and let the company's accumulated earnings pile up. This will increase its underlying intrinsic value and over time will cause the stock price to go up. Berkshire bought Coca-Cola in 1988 and twenty-seven years later still owns it. It bought its first position in Wells Fargo back in 1990, and not only does it still own it, it continues to add to its position. In that time the underlying value of Coke's and Wells Fargo's businesses has increased, and even though we have seen several bull and bear markets, their stock prices have continued a slow rise, reflecting the increasing value of their underlying businesses. As we said earlier, in the case of Coke, Berkshire's $1.299 billion 1988 investment in Coke is now worth $17.184 billion, giving Berkshire an average annual compounding rate of return of 10.04%, not including dividends. Its original investment in 5 million shares of Wells Fargo stock at a total price of $289 million in 1990 has grown to 40 million shares because of stock splits and is worth approximately $1.9 billion, giving Berkshire a 7.5% annual compounding rate of return.

CORPORATE MERGERS

–

"When you mix raisins with turds, you still have turds."

–

Here Charlie is talking about companies buying other companies. If a great company buys a turd of a company, it ends up with a mixture and the turd of a company drags down the results of the great company. A perfect example of this "mixing raisins with turds" phenomenon was when Coca-Cola bought its way into the moviemaking business. Another example was when Gulf and Western Industries bought its way into the moviemaking business. An even better example was when Matsushita Electric bought its way into the moviemaking business. And the best example of all was when Seagram, the Canadian distiller, bought its way into the moviemaking business. (Do you see a pattern developing here?) For those great companies the solution to their problem of mixing a great business with a turd of a business was to flush the turd of the business—which usually meant selling off the movie business to some other starstruck CEO. Charlie might have put it better if he had said that when we mix caviar with turds, all we are going to taste is the turds.

GOING TO EXTREMES

–

"In business we often find that the winning system goes almost ridiculously far in maximizing and or minimizing one or a few variables—like the discount warehouses of Costco."

–

Costco is obsessed with keeping operating costs to a minimum. It does not provide shopping bags—customers bring their own bags or use an empty packing box the store supplies—saving Costco 2 to 5 cents each on plastic bags and 10 to 25 cents each on paper ones. That might not seem significant, but consider this: Costco does $15 billion in sales a year. If the average customer spends $100 per shopping trip, that means that Costco has approximately 150 million customer checkouts every year. If three paper bags at 10 cents per bag were used per checkout, the total bag cost per checkout of 30 cents, multiplied by 150 million, would cost Costco approximately $45 million a year. By simply by getting rid of paper bags at checkout, Costco arguably saves itself $45 million a year.

GEICO did something that seemed outrageous—early on it got rid of the insurance agent and his commission by selling directly to the consumer—thereby reducing its costs, which allowed it to be more competitive in the pricing of its insurance products and still maintain its profit margins.

Bank of America made the extreme decision to focus in on the individual depositor, who had been sorely neglected by larger banks. As the population base of California grew in size and wealth, Bank of America's individual depositors also grew in size and wealth. As a result, today Bank of America is one of the largest banks in the nation.

Unlike its competitors, Berkshire Hathaway's Nebraska Furniture Mart buys huge quantities of furniture from a single manufacturer, at a huge discount, which allows its stores to sell us a sofa cheaper than the competition and still keep its margins high.

The one thing that all of Berkshire's businesses have in common is that they are managed by people who are willing to go to great lengths to keep costs low. That goes for Berkshire's home office as well—it doesn't have a public relations or investor services department, and for many years the annual report was printed on the cheapest paper possible and had no expensive color photos. (Note: In recent years the paper quality has improved and the annual report now sports one color photo—which may be a sign that management is starting to slip.)

BIG-MONEY EQUATION

–

"A great business at a fair price is superior to a fair business at a great price."

–

Okay, let's take a look at the numbers that explain what Charlie is talking about here. Let's say you have $100,000 to invest and you have the choice of investing in either Company A or Company B.

Company A is earning $1 a share, growing its earnings at 15% per year, and selling at 20 times earnings, which equates to $20 a share (20 × $1 = $20). This means that for $100,000 you will be able to buy 5,000 shares of Company A ($100,000 ÷ $20 = 5,000).

Company B, on the other hand, also earns $1 a share but is growing its earnings at 8% per year and is selling at 10 times earnings, or $10 a share. This means that for $100,000 you can buy 10,000 shares of Company B ($100,000 ÷ $10 = 10,000).

At first blush it looks as though Company B is the better buy. It earns $1 a share and it is selling for $10 a share, which equates to a price-to-earnings ratio of only 10. Company A, which is also earning $1 a share, is selling at a pricy 20 times earnings or $20 a share, which is twice what Company B is selling for. But if we take a look at it from a ten-year perspective, the projected results present a completely different story.

In ten years Company B's earnings, growing at 8% a year, will have grown to $2.19 a share. If the company's shares are still trading at 10 times earnings, this equates to a per share price of $21.90 ($2.19 × 10 = $21.90), which gives us a profit of $11.90 a share ($21.90 − $10 per share cost = $11.90 per share profit). Multiply $11.90 a share profit by the 10,000 shares we own, and we show a total net profit of $119,000 on our original $100,000 investment in Company B.

However, Company A's earnings, growing at 15% a year, will have grown to $4.05 a share by year ten. If the company's shares are still trading at 20 times earnings, this equates to a price of $81 per share (20 × $4.05 = $81), which equates to a profit of $61 a share ($81 − $20 a share cost = $61 a share profit). Multiply the $61 per share profit by the 5,000 shares we own, and we show a total net profit of $305,000 on our original $100,000 investment in Company A.

Company A, the better business, selling at a fair price, will make us $186,000 more than an investment in Company B, the fair business selling at what initially appears to be a bargain price ($305,000 − $119,000 = $186,000). In the old days, before Warren met Charlie, he would have bought Company B. But after Warren met Charlie he became a Company A man with all his heart and soul. Just remember: "A great business at a fair price is superior to a fair business at a great price." It worked well for Charlie and Warren, and it will work for you as well.

TWO KINDS OF BUSINESSES

–

*"There are two kinds of businesses: The first earns 12%,
and you can take it out at the end of the year. The second
earns 12%, but all the excess cash must be reinvested—
there's never any cash. It reminds me of the guy who
looks at all of his equipment and says, 'There's all of my
profit.' We hate that kind of business."*

–

Early in Charlie's career as an investor he got involved in a high-tech
business that was manufacturing sophisticated measuring devices for
science. The company had good sales, but every dollar it earned had to
go right back into the business. Luckily for Charlie, he sold the company
right before the technology changed and rendered the company's product
obsolete. He had the same experience with Berkshire's textile business:
in good times it made money, even created a small surplus, but as time
went on the textile business became so competitive that every dollar
the company made had to be spent trying to keep the business afloat.

Charlie had the exact opposite experience with See's Candies—the
pots that hold the chocolate were fifty years old and still didn't need
replacing, and the product was the same year after year. The business
required very little in capital expenditures, so it was possible to take
money out of it every year to invest in other businesses.

FEW COMPANIES SURVIVE

–

"Over the very long term, history shows that the chances of any business surviving in a manner agreeable to a company's owners are slim at best."

–

Most businesses eventually change and many do die; that has been true for a great many industrial, transportation, and communication businesses. Blue Chip Stamp was a great business when Berkshire first bought it the 1960s, but today it is no longer in existence. When Berkshire bought Dexter Shoe Company in 1993, Warren was singing to shareholders, "There's no business like the shoe business." That was true until Dexter Shoe, which manufactured its shoes in the United States, could no longer compete with foreign manufacturers that had access to cheaper labor. The *Washington Post* was once one of the most influential and profitable newspapers in the United States, but in a mere ten years the Internet decimated its business model. Since 1960 more than forty car manufacturers alone have called it quits. Do you remember DeLorean? How about Edsel? Or Saab? All of them have gone off to that great big used-car lot in the sky, never to be heard from again.

SEE'S CANDIES

—

"When we bought See's Candy, we didn't know the power of a good brand. Over time, we just discovered that we could raise prices 10% a year and no one cared. Learning that changed Berkshire. It was really important."

—

Charlie learned that with certain products one can raise prices and demand doesn't drop. Most of the things we buy in life are commodities. They are interchangeable: a steak from butcher X is similar to a steak from butcher Y. The gas we buy from one station is the same as the gas from another station. As a result the competition between butchers and gas stations is based on price. That makes it very hard to raise prices. But some brand-name products own a piece of consumers' minds and don't have any direct competition. When Charlie and Warren first discovered such companies, they called them "consumer monopolies." See's Candies is one of those consumer monopolies. See's has made candy on the same machinery year after year, which has meant low capital expenditures, and because its product brand owns a piece of consumers' minds, it can slowly raise prices without hurting demand. That equates to higher margins on sales, which means that See's makes more money on each piece of candy it sells. That means See's can keep its pricing in pace with inflation; it also means that the return on Berkshire's original investment keeps growing year after year. Consider this: When Berkshire bought See's in 1972 for $25 million, the company had a net income of $4.2 million a year. In 2007 Berkshire reported that See's earned Berkshire $82 million, which means net earnings have risen at a compounding annual rate of 8.6% a year. In 2011, Berkshire reported that in forty years of ownership See's has earned Berkshire a staggering $1.65 billion in profits.

This little bit of knowledge has had a great impact on Berkshire and was an integral part of the buying equation it used to buy Coca-Cola. Though Coke doesn't have quite the pricing freedom of See's, it does own a piece of consumers' minds and is able to raise prices to keep up with inflation. When Berkshire bought its Coca-Cola stock in 1988, the company had a net income of $1.03 billion. Thirty years later, in 2015, Coca-Cola reported a net income of $7.3 billion, giving it a 608% increase in earnings, which equates to an average annual increase of 20.2% and an average annual compounding growth rate of 6.75%.

With See's Charlie and Warren had finally found the Holy Grail of investments: a company that has an ever-increasing underlying value. And to unlock that value all they had to do was hold the investment for as long as possible.

EASY DECISIONS/
PAINFUL DECISIONS

–

"The difference between a good business and a bad business is that good businesses throw up one easy decision after another. The bad businesses throw up painful decisions time after time."

–

A lifetime of investing and owning companies has taught Charlie and Warren many lessons. They have both owned a few bad businesses in their day: a department store, a windmill manufacturer, a textile factory, and an airline. Why are those businesses bad? Because they are involved in intensely competitive industries that beat each other up over price, which brings their profit margins down, kills their cash flow, and diminishes their chances of long-term survivability. But Charlie and Warren's education in misery has been our gain. Now we know that the secret is always to go with the better business that has a durable competitive advantage and can raise prices at will. This allows it to keep its margins high, which creates lots of free cash flow to spend on new business opportunities.

MARKET DECLINES

—

"If you're not willing to react with equanimity to a market price decline of 50% two or three times a century you're not fit to be a common shareholder and you deserve the mediocre result you're going to get compared to the people who do have the temperament, who can be more philosophical about these market fluctuations."

—

In the fifty years that Charlie has owned Berkshire Hathaway stock he has seen its stock price fall by 50% three separate times. If he had sold his shares during any one of those declines his net worth would be a fraction of what it is today. Charlie believes that it is the nature of long-term stock holding to occasionally experience a steep decline in a share price, which in Berkshire's case it has always fully recovered from. But this phenomenon of decline and recovery has more to do with the economic nature of the company than the price fluctuation of the stock. Let me explain: The great stock market crashes of 1929 and 1932 devastated stock prices drastically, and the Dow Jones Industrial Average didn't fully recover until 1954. It took twenty-five years for the DJIA to return to its precrash highs. However, companies with excellent economics working in their favor, the ones with a durable competitive advantage, such as Coca-Cola and Philip Morris, returned to their precrash highs by 1936. The mediocre companies, the ones with the poor business economics, took as long as twenty-five years before things started to look bright again. Charlie has never had to wait that long. Why? Because he invests only in companies with excellent economics working in their favor, such as the Coca-Cola Company and Berkshire Hathaway, which will quickly recover from any stock market crash.

WHERE TO PLACE OUR BET

—

"Averaged out, betting on the quality of a business is better than betting on the quality of management . . . but, very rarely, you find a manager who's so good that you're wise to follow him into what looks like a mediocre business."

—

This reminds me of the story of Mrs. B's Warehouse. Mrs. B started the Nebraska Furniture Mart in Omaha, Nebraska, in 1937. She grew it into the most successful furniture store in the United States. Berkshire bought 90% of the company from her when she was eighty-nine years old, and she stayed on, managing it with her sons. Five years later she got into a fight with her sons, left in a huff, and started a new store across the street. What harm can a ninety-four-year-old woman do to a multibillion-dollar conglomerate owned and run by a couple of business geniuses? In no time at all she had taken so much of Nebraska Furniture Mart's business that Berkshire was forced to spend millions of dollars buying her out a second time. But this time around they had her sign a noncompete clause, a very wise thing to do given that she went on to work seven days a week, open to close, till she passed away at the age of 104. But as a general rule, bet on the quality of the business, not on the quality of the management—unless, of course, you've got a Mrs. B. in your hand. If that is the case, go all in.

INCENTIVES

–

"From all business, my favorite case on incentives is Federal Express. The heart and soul of their system— which creates the integrity of the product—is having all their airplanes come to one place in the middle of the night and shift all the packages from plane to plane. If there are delays, the whole operation can't deliver a product full of integrity to Federal Express customers. And it was always screwed up. They could never get it done on time. They tried everything—moral suasion, threats, you name it. And nothing worked. Finally, some- body got the idea to pay all these people not so much an hour, but so much a shift—and when it's all done, they can go home. Well, their problems cleared up overnight."

–

Here Charlie is talking about incentives. All of us who have held hourly jobs know that if workers are paid by the hour they will work more slowly than if they are paid them by the job. Why? Because if they are paid by the hour, they have an incentive to work more slowly in order to put more hours on the clock and make more money. But if they are paid by the job, there is an incentive to work quickly so they can get onto the next job and make more money. Federal Express aligned management's goals with employee incentives. With hourly pay their employees were never in a hurry, but when pay was given for a specific task—getting a plane loaded—suddenly they were in a rush to get the job done. The key wasn't paying workers by the task or shift; the key was letting them go home if they finished early, which was a kind of financial reward in that they were getting paid for the full shift even if they left early.

AIG AND GE

–

"AIG is a lot like GE. It is a fabulously successful insurance operator, and with success it morphed into a massive carry business—borrowing a lot of money at one price and investing it at another price. AIG was a big operator that was a lot like GE Credit. We never owned either because even the best and wisest people make us nervous in great big credit operations with swollen balance sheets. It just makes me nervous, that many people borrowing so many billions."

–

Well, it turned out that Charlie was right, the carry trade nearly bankrupted both AIG and GE in 2007–09. And in 2015 GE began the process of selling off its financial division. Borrowing short term at cheap rates and lending it out long term at higher rates is an easy way to make tons of money as long as one can keep rolling over the short-term loans at cheap rates. But if short-term interest rates climb above what the money was borrowed at or the bankers decide not to roll over the short-term loans, the whole thing collapses like a house of cards. GE found this out the hard way, which is why it is wishing its financial operations a fond bon voyage.

LESS LEVERAGE

—

"As you can tell in Berkshire's operations, we are much more conservative. We borrow less, on more favorable terms. We're happier with less leverage. You could argue that we've been wrong, and that it's cost us a fortune, but that doesn't bother us. Missing out on some opportunity never bothers us. What's wrong with someone getting a little richer than you? It's crazy to worry about this."

—

Charlie has learned that leverage and envy are a lethal combination. Leverage is just another name for debt. The attraction of using leverage (debt) is that it allows one to leverage equity capital to make even more money. However, using leverage not only increases your gain when things go your way; it also increases your losses if things don't. Managers of investment banks love using lots of leverage. As we said earlier, if their leverage bets go as expected, they can justify paying themselves tens of millions of dollars in bonuses. If they lose the bets, they blame the market and hope their trading losses can be covered up by the bank's other operations. However, occasionally the use of leverage causes trading losses so steep that they bankrupt the firm.

How do banks get themselves into this mess? Envy. They see the guys at the other banks making millions, and they want to make big bucks, too. So they keep adding more and more layers of leverage to increase their winnings. How much do they goose them? With a normal commercial bank the FDIC likes to see a debt-to-equity ratio of 10 to 1. When Lehman Brothers went bust, it had a debt-to-equity ratio in the neighborhood of 30 to 1. That had earned it a ton of money, until its fortunes reversed, and then it drove it into bankruptcy.

Charlie and Warren have always avoided using large amounts of leverage/debt with Berkshire. They have also tried to avoid investing in companies that have high debt-to-equity ratios. The net result is that Berkshire has been able to profit off the financial debt-laden folly of others while not partaking in it itself.

MASTER PLANS

—

"At Berkshire there has never been a master plan. Anyone who wanted to do it, we fired because it takes on a life of its own and doesn't cover new reality. We want people taking into account new information."

—

The business world is a dynamic place. Much like a battlefield, it changes rapidly, and no one has thought more about "master plans" being applied to a dynamic setting than the nineteenth-century Prussian military thinker Carl von Clausewitz, who wrote that battle "is a continuous interaction of opposites" in which "my opponent . . . dictates to me as much as I dictate to him." He also wrote that "No war plan outlasts the first encounter with the enemy." But my all-time favorite quote on this subject is by none other than Prussian field marshal Count Helmuth von Moltke, who wrote, "The material and moral consequences of every major battle are so far-reaching that they usually bring about a completely altered situation, a new basis for the adoption of new measures. One cannot be at all sure that any operational plan will survive the first encounter with the main body of the enemy. Only a layman could suppose that the development of a campaign represents the strict application of a prior concept that has been worked out in every detail and followed through to the very end."

That isn't to say that one shouldn't have plans to solve specific problems; one should, but one should follow Charlie's advice and make plans that take into account new information as it develops. And an overall master plan to guide a business for the next ten years is unrealistic on the part of its author and is seldom worth the time and energy spent on it. It is far better to keep things simple and improvise as we go along. Whenever I think of "master plans," I remember Nebraska Furniture Mart's founder, Mrs. B., who, in response to a question about having a business plan, replied in her thick Russian accent, "Yeah, sell cheap and tell the truth." She was a business genius.

DECENTRALIZATION

–

"How is [Berkshire] organized? I don't think in [the] history of the world has anything Berkshire's size [been] organized in so decentralized a fashion."

–

The one thing that Charlie and Warren did that is unique in the world of corporate conglomerates was to dismiss the idea of synergy. What happens, happens, but the heads of each of Berkshire's subsidiaries are free to do business with whomever they want, whenever they want, even if it is a competitor of one of Berkshire's other subsidiaries.

Unlike most corporate conglomerates, Berkshire does not have a quota system imposed by headquarters requiring the subsidiaries to meet HQ's numbers. At Berkshire the CEO running the subsidiary calls the shots and sets the projections.

Berkshire's culture is also unique in that it will let businesses run out, which means that instead of selling a subsidiary with declining revenue and future prospects, it will keep on running the business until it's time to shut the doors, as we did with Berkshire's textile operations. There is no discarding a wholly owned Berkshire subsidiary company because it is doing poorly, as CEO Jack Welch used to do at General Electric.

This strategy of decentralization almost to the point of abdication frees Berkshire's subsidiary managers—the people with the best knowledge—to adapt their businesses to the economic environment as they see fit, without being meddled with by a less knowledgeable home office. It also allows Charlie and Warren to avoid the financial costs and inefficiencies of running a large corporate bureaucracy. Sometimes less really is more.

ENRON

—

"The people who carry the torch in accounting are in a noble profession, yet these people also gave us Enron."

—

Enron was an energy, commodities, and transmission company that posted revenues of $111 billion in the year 2000. *Fortune* magazine had named Enron the nation's most innovative company six years in a row. In 2001 it came out that one of Enron's greatest innovations was creatively planned accounting fraud. Essentially the company had been goosing its net earnings by shifting massive investment losses off Enron's balance sheet by dumping them into offshore partnerships. Enron was insolvent and had been for a long time, but with the help of its accounting firm, Arthur Andersen, it was able to fool investors, banks, and the general public for many years. When the fraud was revealed, there were criminal charges against the officers of the company, Enron was put into bankruptcy, and there were lawsuits against both the company and its accounting firm. As a result, Arthur Andersen was dissolved.

What was most shocking was that Arthur Andersen, one of the nation's top accounting firms at the time, had been complicit in the acts of fraud. Sometimes really smart people can do really stupid things.

GM

—

"Berkshire is in GM because one of our young men likes it. Warren, when he was a young man, got to do whatever he wanted to do, and that's the way it is. It is true GM may be protected by the federal government in the end, and it may be a good investment in the end, but the industry is as competitive as I've ever seen. Everyone can make good cars, they have the same suppliers, and cars last forever. It just has all these commoditized features. So I don't think the auto industry is the place to be."

—

One of the Berkshire portfolio mysteries in recent years has been: Why did the company buy into GM? The auto industry is a highly competitive business that produces a product that has a lot of price competition—and although there are years when GM makes lots of money, it also has a history of years with big losses. When *Buffettology* was written back in 1996, I talked about GM manufacturing a commodity-type product and how it had never really made its investors any money; it had a history of boom and bust. In 2007 a bust caught up with GM, and it lost $38 billion. In the following year, 2008, it lost $30 billion. When GM filed for Chapter 11 bankruptcy in 2009, it had $82 billion in assets and $172 billion in debt, making it insolvent to the tune of $90 billion, which completely wiped out its shareholders.

The federal government injected $50 billion into a new entity, which bought the old GM's assets. In 2015 the new GM reported earnings of $9.6 billion, with total assets of $194 billion and total liabilities of $63 billion, giving it a comfortable cushion of $131 billion in assets. Today, GM seems like a completely new being, except for one thing: it is still manufacturing a commodity-type product in a highly competitive industry. One of Berkshire's new investment managers may think it is a good long-term bet, but Charlie still doesn't think the auto business is the place to be.

ISCAR

–

"We didn't know when we were young which things to stretch for, but by the time we reached Iscar, which we never would have bought when we were young, we knew to stretch for the right people. It's a hell of a business. Everything is right there. Isn't it good that we keep learning? Better late than never."

–

Iscar is an Israel-based, worldwide maker of precision carbide metal-cutting tools used in industry. It is the dominant player in its field. Berkshire purchased 80% of the company in 2006 for $4 billion and then purchased the final 20% in 2013 for $2 billion—which shows that it was a better business in 2013 than it was in 2006. Iscar was the first whole company Berkshire purchased outside the United States. Benjamin Graham would have never bought it because it wasn't selling below book value—his idea of a bargain. Charlie and Warren learned with the purchase of Nebraska Furniture Mart that if the dominant player is large enough and well enough entrenched with its customer base, the cost of entry into its market is much too high for potential competitors. Size and market domination can create their own kind of durable competitive advantage, which is what Iscar has in spades.

WELLS FARGO

—

"Even the best banks drift with the times and do stupid things, but I suspect Wells Fargo will face up to it better."

—

Here Charlie is saying that Wells Fargo will do stupid bank things as well, just not as many and hopefully not as big as, say, Citicorp has done in the past. But this goes back to the emphasis on the quality of the management, its integrity, and its ability to keep its eye on the ball. Even Wells Fargo's total derivatives exposure of $5 trillion is tiny compared to JPMorgan Chase's $63 trillion, Citicorp's $60 trillion, and Goldman's $57 trillion. Which tells us that the next time the derivatives market implodes, Wells Fargo may be the last big bank left standing.

MCDONALD'S

–

"This is a nice college, but the really great educator is McDonald's. . . . I think a lot of what goes on there is better than at Harvard."

–

A chain is only as strong as its weakest link, and it doesn't matter how strong the strongest links are if they are connected to the weakest ones. What Charlie is saying here is that McDonald's is improving the strength of our culture's weakest links by hiring people with bad work habits, giving them training, and teaching them good work habits such as coming to work on time and how to deal with customers in a pleasant manner. It can take credit for teaching literally millions of America's young people good work habits over the sixty years since it opened its doors. And since McDonald's is in 118 countries and employs more than 1.7 million people around the globe, we might argue that it is doing so for young people all over the world. That is one hell of an accomplishment that not even Harvard can lay claim to.

LIQUIDITY

–

"After the South Sea Bubble, Britain outlawed public corporations—only private ones allowed. And they led the world for 100 years. A modest amount of liquidity will serve the situation. Too much liquidity will hurt human nature. I would never be tenured if I said that. But I'm right and they are wrong."

–

The South Sea Bubble is a reference to the South Sea Company, which was a British joint-stock company formed in 1711 to help reduce England's national debt. (It wasn't till World War I that England discovered deficit financing via running the central bank's printing presses.) The British government, after payoffs to many members of Parliament, granted South Sea a monopoly to conduct trade with South America. At the prospect of the riches that would come from its trading monopoly and its dealings in government debt, the company became the most popular stock of its day, with the share prices rising far above what the company was intrinsically worth. When earnings didn't materialize, the stock price collapsed and many people, including nobles, lost their fortunes. In response to the South Sea Bubble bursting, England enacted the Bubble Act of 1720, which forbade the formation of a joint-stock company without a royal charter, and the chartered companies weren't allowed to be publicly traded. For the next hundred years England led the world in commerce.

Which brings us to the question of liquidity. Liquidity is the measure of how easy it is to turn assets into cash, in this case how easy it is to sell shares for cash. The more active the market there is for certain shares, the more liquid those shares are. One of the arguments made by Wall Street for derivatives is that they increase liquidity—but at what cost, and is that cost ultimately worth it? Charlie thinks not.

SINGAPORE

–

"In a democracy, everyone takes turns. But if you really want a lot of wisdom, it's better to concentrate decisions and process in one person. It's no accident that Singapore has a much better record, given where it started, than the United States. There, power was concentrated in an enormously talented person, Lee Kuan Yew, who was the Warren Buffett of Singapore."

–

I think it is best to start with a quote from Lee Kuan Yew himself: "With few exceptions, democracy has not brought good government to new developing countries. . . . What Asians value may not necessarily be what Americans or Europeans value. Westerners value the freedoms and liberties of the individual. As an Asian of Chinese cultural background, my values are for a government which is honest, effective, and efficient." And as prime minister of Singapore from 1959 to 1990 he did just that: he created a government that was honest, effective, and efficient.

To help keep government employees honest, Lee paid them what they could make in the private sector. To spur economic growth, he courted multinational corporations to build manufacturing plants in Singapore by giving them tax breaks and helping them get financing.

To help new businesses raise capital, he turned Singapore into an international financial center by creating favorable banking laws and providing a stable currency. To facilitate dealings with the two most powerful financial centers of the world at the time, New York and London, he instituted English as the national language. In response, US companies such as Texas Instruments, Hewlett-Packard, and General Electric built their first Asian manufacturing plants in Singapore.

The key to it all was providing an honest, effective, and efficient government to provide businesses with the stable, uncorrupt, working environment they needed to grow and prosper. In the process Singapore went from being a third-world country to being a twenty-first-century world financial and manufacturing center. Lee's book *From Third World to First: The Singapore Story* is well worth a read. Charlie became so enamored of Lee that he commissioned a bronze bust of him to keep the one he owns of Benjamin Franklin company.

PART IV

–

CHARLIE'S ADVICE ON LIFE, EDUCATION, AND THE PURSUIT OF HAPPINESS

ONE STEP AT A TIME

–

"Spend each day trying to be a little wiser than you were when you woke up. Discharge your duties faithfully and well. Slug it out one inch at a time, day by day. At the end of the day—if you live long enough—most people get what they deserve."

–

This is Charlie's incremental approach to getting ahead in life, which is similar to the childhood parable of the race between the tortoise and the hare. For those of us who don't remember, the hare, who is infinitely faster, loses the race to the much slower, but more consistent tortoise, who keeps plugging along one inch at a time. In Charlie's own life, when he was practicing law, he implemented a self-education regime for one hour a day to learn such things as real estate development and stock investing. It was slow going at first, but after a great number of years and thousands of books read, he started to see how different areas of knowledge interplay with each other and how knowledge, like money, can compound, making one more and more aware of the world in which he or she lives. He has often said that he is a much better investor at ninety than he was at fifty, a fact he attributes to the compounding effect of knowledge.

WHAT WE DESERVE

–

"The best way to get a good spouse is to deserve a good spouse."

–

What I think Charlie is saying here is that in matters of the heart, we tend to get what we deserve. Good people tend to find other good people to walk down the aisle with, just as bad people tend to marry people equally as negative. He has applied this theory to the business world by making Berkshire a good and trusted steward of the wonderful companies it buys. He attracts business owners who want to sell their much-loved businesses to him. Quality attracts quality, be it in business or in marriage.

USING BIG IDEAS

–

*"Know the big ideas in the big disciplines and use them
routinely—all of them, not just a few."*

–

Charlie is a graduate of Harvard Law School, studied meteorology at
the California Institute of Technology, and is well read in the areas
of psychology, science, economics, and history. How does he use
this knowledge in the investment world?

If you understand psychology, you can grasp how a product such
as Coca-Cola can own a piece of consumers' minds—which makes
it a candidate for a long-term investment.

If you have a grasp of science, you can appreciate that the
fast-changing world of computer technology might not be the most
stable environment for a long-term investment.

In the banking crisis of 2007–09, Charlie, having studied central banking, knew that if the Fed nationalized the banks, in effect
becoming their new owner, it would have essentially wiped out all
the shareholders' equity, which would have caused investors to flee
all the banks, making it impossible for even the best of banks to
raise new equity capital. He knew that the safest and most rational
course for the Fed to take was to infuse new capital into the troubled
banks by buying their preferred shares, which is a kind of debt that

is carried on the bank's balance sheet as equity but that doesn't dilute shareholders' ownership interests. So as we said earlier, in 2008, when banks' stocks were getting hammered on fears that the Fed would have to nationalize them, Charlie was loading up on Wells Fargo at $8.58 a share. Today Wells Fargo trades around $47 a share. But if he had never studied how central banks such as the Fed work, he would have joined the great mass of fearful investors jumping ship, instead of making the buy of a lifetime.

CAREER ADVICE

–

"Three rules for a career: (1) Don't sell anything you wouldn't buy yourself; (2) Don't work for anyone you don't respect and admire; and (3) Work only with people you enjoy."

–

Career advice from Charlie is always a gift. Why don't we sell things we would never buy? Because every book ever written on selling says that if we don't like, understand, or believe in a product, we are going to be a disaster when we try to sell it. Great salespeople believe in their products. That is one of the secrets of their success.

Why don't we work for people we don't respect? Because they have nothing to teach us and cannot help us advance our intellect and life.

Why shouldn't we work with people we don't enjoy? Because work is our life, and one of the measures of living a rich life is enjoying what we do and who we spend time with. If we are miserable at work, even if we are making millions, it is a poorly lived life.

KNOW-IT-ALLS

—

"I try to get rid of people who always confidently answer questions about which they don't have any real knowledge."

—

The problem here is one of trust. If people don't have the integrity to admit when they don't know something, how can one ever trust them? It is much better to jettison such a person and find someone with a bit more intellectual honesty. Again, Charlie shows that he is as interested in knowing what is unknown as in knowing what is known. The opinion of someone who can't tell the difference is useless.

A WASTE OF EDUCATION

–

"A big percentage of Caltech grads are going into finance. . . . They'll make a lot of money by clobbering customers who aren't as smart as them. It's a mistake. I look at this in terms of losses from the diversion of our best talent going into some money-grubbing exercise."

–

Once upon a time Caltech was one of the greatest science and engineering schools in the world. It is the home of NASA's Jet Propulsion Laboratory. Charlie studied there back in the 1940s. In 2010 the big money being made gambling on Wall Street packaged derivatives was too enticing to Caltech's professors and students, who began shifting their energies and focus from subjects such as space exploration and advanced computer technology to designing sophisticated mathematical models to help Wall Street trading desks make investment banks even more money. From Charlie's perspective the best and brightest young minds should be engineering solutions to solve the world's problems, not squandering their intellects on finding better ways to win a game of chance in a Wall Street casino.

ADMITTING STUPIDITY

—

"I like people admitting they were complete stupid horses' asses. I know I'll perform better if I rub my nose in my mistakes. This is a wonderful trick to learn."

—

Charlie believes that we can learn from our failures only if we accept responsibility for them and examine exactly why we failed. Blaming someone else and shirking responsibility is a missed learning opportunity. That is why Berkshire's annual report is always quick to point out Warren and Charlie's screw-ups and the lessons they learned—such as their investment in US Airways, which they thought going in was a good investment but proved to be a real stinker. This "nose-rubbing" exercise is one reason why they never make the same mistake twice.

MAKING MISTAKES

–

"There's no way that you can live an adequate life without many mistakes. In fact, one trick in life is to get so you can handle mistakes. Failure to handle psychological denial is a common way for people to go broke."

–

It's comforting to hear—that it's okay to make a mistake. Charlie is a better investor today because he rode a bull market way too long and got slaughtered in the crash of 1973–74. He is also a better investor because of the problems Berkshire faced after it purchased Dexter Shoe. And let's not forget the nightmare Charlie had with Salomon Brothers, which almost cost Berkshire its entire $700 million investment in the company. Then there were problems with the Baltimore department store Hochschild Kohn and, as we said, US Airlines. Those were huge mistakes in business judgment, often costing millions of dollars. But they set the stage for a greatly improved investment strategy that later paid off in billions.

SPECIALIZATION

–

"Extreme specialization is the way to succeed. Most people are way better off specializing than trying to understand the world."

–

Specialization is the key to survival in any species, and it is the key to success in any business. Specialization protects us from the competition. Why? Because specialization presents a barrier of entry to the competition—and the more difficult it is to become specialized, the greater the barrier. If all we do is what everyone else does, we will spend our lives competing head on with everyone else. But if we specialize in something and excel at it, the specialization will set us apart from the rest of the crowd. Do we take our Porsche to the local car mechanic who works on everyone's car? Of course not. We take it to the shop that specializes in Porsches. It charges us twice the normal hourly rate and gets away with it because it is a "Porsche specialist." The same phenomenon holds true for medicine, law, and even the trades, such as plumbing and carpentry. It's specialists who make the big bucks—everyone else, the little bucks.

NOT WORKING

–

"It's been my experience in life, if you just keep thinking and reading, you don't have to work."

–

Tired of that dead-end Wall Street job? Boss getting you down? Your derivatives book about to blow up and end your lucrative career? Just keep thinking and reading, and you will be all right. Why? Because that is all there is to the investment game from Charlie's point of view: you think a lot, and you read a lot. It's said that Charlie reads up to six hundred pages a day—which includes three newspapers a day and a weekly diet of several books. Oh yes, and occasionally he goes out to the Los Angeles Country Club for a club sandwich and a Coke. This is a guy who knows how to splurge in between power reads.

NOT LIVING BEYOND OUR MEANS

—

"Mozart is a good example of a life ruined by nuttiness. His achievement wasn't diminished—he may well have had the best innate musical talent ever—but from the start, he was pretty miserable. He overspent his income his entire life—that will make you miserable."

—

One of the keys to Charlie's accumulation of wealth is that in his youth he was fanatical about not spending money. He didn't buy his first new car until he was almost sixty, and he lived in an upper-middle-class house long after he became a multimillionaire. Every dollar saved was a dollar that could be invested. Overspending can make us miserable, but underspending and investing wisely will help speed us along the road to riches.

OUT WITH THE OLD

–

"Any year that passes in which you don't destroy one of your best loved ideas is a wasted year."

–

Out with the old and in with the new. This shows an evolution in our thought process, which means we are actually thinking. What Charlie is saying is that in any year we haven't tossed out one of our best-loved ideas, it probably means we aren't reading and thinking enough to evolve a little bit further in our intellectual development. In the investment game, throwing out a well-loved investment idea can happen with some regularity. The world of business is a dynamic environment that can experience radical change over a very short period of time. In a mere seventy years the United States went from no electricity to the entire country being electrified. That completely destroyed candle making, gas lighting, and the kerosene lamp businesses, all great enterprises in the eighteenth and nineteenth centuries. In 1930 there weren't any televisions in people's homes. By 1960 just about every American home had one, and the home radio business, the Internet of the 1920s, pretty much died. In 2000 there wasn't such a thing as *Wikipedia*. Today we can't live without it, and *Wikipedia* killed the 244-year-old encyclopedia business—which had been a really good business. In 1974 the digital camera didn't exist.

OUT WITH THE OLD

Today Kodak doesn't exist—and for a hundred years previously Kodak had been an amazingly successful business! In the world of business and investing it is best to keep up with new developments and review our best-loved ideas every year, just to make sure that in thinking we are right, we don't get it wrong.

A MORAL IMPERATIVE

—

"Being rational is a moral imperative. You should never be stupider than you need to be."

—

This is Charlie's twist on Immanuel Kant, the eighteenth-century German philosopher, who argued that reason is the source of all morality. Being rational, to Kant and Charlie, means ignoring our emotions, and following logic and reason in making our decisions (sounds a lot like Charlie talking about making a stock purchase). A "moral imperative" is a strongly felt principle originating inside a person's mind that compels that person to act or not act; and according to Kant and Charlie, to do otherwise would be self-defeating and thus contrary to reason. In Charlie's world, not being rational is the same as being stupid.

SECRET OF SUCCESS

—

"I have never succeeded very much in anything in which I was not very interested. If you can't somehow find yourself very interested in something, I don't think you'll succeed very much, even if you're fairly smart."

—

Charlie often says that the key to being a great business manager is to have a passion for the business. For people who have that, the business isn't a job, it's the love of their lives. They would rather be at work than at home. They are artists whose passion for their work drives and defines their lives. Here Charlie is pointing out that this theory applies to anything we do in life: To be successful in something, we need to be passionately interested in it. And that passion, more than raw intelligence, tends to determine whether or not we will be successful at what we do. As Steve Jobs said, "Work is going to fill a large part of your life, and the only way to be truly satisfied is to do what you believe is great work. And the only way to do great work is to love what you do."

BEING FRUGAL

—

"One of the great defenses—if you're worried about inflation—is not to have a lot of silly needs in your life—if you don't need a lot of material goods."

—

Both Charlie and Warren have lived in upper-middle-class homes and driven older-model cars most of their lives. Why? To keep their expenses low, so that they could accumulate lots of cash to invest. How does this protect them against inflation? If you don't need something, you don't have to buy it—so who cares if it goes up in price? Do you really think Charlie has ever lost sleep over the ever-increasing price of a new Ferrari?

IDEOLOGY

—

"Another thing I think should be avoided is extremely intense ideology because it cabbages up one's mind."

—

Charlie believes that youth is easily influenced and often becomes obsessed with an ideology to the point that it is impossible to think of anything else or to see another side of an argument. Passion blinds young people to any kind of rational thought process.

From an investing perspective, it was only with Charlie's help that Warren broke his chains of habit and ideology and finally set aside the Graham approach of investing in mediocre companies at bargain prices. He began to invest in great companies at fair prices and holding them forever. Older men, like passionate youths, can become so wedded to an ideology that it stops them from seeing a better way. Which is why it is a good thing to have a guy like Charlie Munger as your friend and business partner.

IDEA DESTRUCTION

–

"We all are learning, modifying, or destroying ideas all the time. Rapid destruction of your ideas when the time is right is one of the most valuable qualities you can acquire. You must force yourself to consider arguments on the other side."

–

This sounds easy, but it is very difficult to put into practice. People don't like to give up long-held ideas. Doing so makes them uncomfortable and fills them with fear. And change usually requires an enormous amount of work. Probably the hardest "idea destruction" thought process that Charlie and Warren ever went through was the closing of Berkshire Hathaway's textile business. Even when it became apparent that the business didn't have a future and would never make any real money, they still kept it open. Only when the business started to really lose money did they finally face the music and close it.

Another example was Charlie and Warren's investment in the Baltimore department store Hochschild Kohn, which they bought at a bargain price and soon realized was a lousy business. It took them nearly three years to find someone to take it off their hands. When it comes to selling an investment, companies that aren't publicly traded are the toughest to get rid of.

The simple lesson here is that Charlie's mind is never standing still. He does not rest on his laurels, and neither should we.

CATECHISM

—

"Oh, it's just so useful dealing with people you can trust and getting all the others the hell out of your life. It ought to be taught as a catechism. . . . But wise people want to avoid other people who are just total rat poison, and there are a lot of them."

—

A catechism is the summary of a doctrine that is used to teach young students, usually religious instruction. What Charlie is advocating here is a philosophy that says we need to jettison our least trustworthy friends and business associates. This has lots of implications. First on a personal level, let's just say that large family gatherings might become a thing of the past if one were to no longer associate with untrustworthy family members. In the business world, not being able to trust your employees or a counterparty in a transaction may result in a tremendous amount of anxiety and inefficiency because trust is the grease that keeps every business running smoothly. If you own a trucking company or operate a hospital, your managers must trust their employees to execute their jobs effectively and trust that the products and materials they order will be delivered on time. If this is not possible, the company is in deep trouble.

COOKIE-CUTTER SOLUTIONS

–

" 'One solution fits all' is not the way to go. . . . The right culture for the Mayo Clinic is different from the right culture at a Hollywood movie studio. You can't run all these places with a cookie-cutter solution."

–

Charlie is talking about organizational structures and the dynamics of how management and employees interact among themselves and with their customers. His experience tells him that businesses are all unique, that we can't take one structure that works for one business and expect it to work with another. When Berkshire Hathaway buys a business, it generally leaves the existing culture intact and is very reluctant to change it. Berkshire's managers stay with the same division or company for life. The great managers on the insurance side of Berkshire are never sent over to the railroad side and vice versa. Companies such as General Electric, on the other hand, will often take a great manager in one division or company and send him or her to a completely different one. Charlie has attributed this reluctance to shifting Berkshire's managers around to be one of the reasons why Berkshire went from being a tiny textile manufacturer to eventually outgrowing General Electric in size.

LEARNING MACHINES

–

"Warren is one of the best learning machines on this earth. . . . Warren's investing skills have markedly increased since he turned 65. Having watched the whole process with Warren, I can report that if he had stopped with what he knew at earlier points, the record would be a pale shadow of what it is."

–

Warren got to be a much better investor after turning sixty-five, which means that there is hope for almost everyone regardless of age. It pays big to keep on learning well after we hit retirement, especially in the investment game. There is another point that I've noticed with men and women who truly excel at their craft or profession: they keep on learning and improving themselves long after most people would have retired. It's like sharks. They have to swim to live; learning is just something those people have to do.

SECRET TO WISDOM

–

"Look at this generation, with all of its electronic devices and multitasking. I will confidently predict less success than Warren, who just focused on reading. If you want wisdom, you'll get it sitting on your ass. That's the way it comes."

–

Reading personal biographies allows one to experience multiple lives and successes and failures; reading business biographies allows one to experience the vicissitudes of a business and learn how problems were solved. Both Charlie and Warren are copious readers of personal and business biographies. I might add that if Charlie ever wrote an autobiography it would probably be titled "How I Read My Way to Fame and Fortune—While Sitting on My Ass."

LEGAL BUSINESS

—

"The best legal experience I ever got was when I was very young. I asked my father why he did so much work for a big blowhard, an overreaching jerk, rather than for his best friend Grant McFadden. He said, 'That man you call a blowhard is a walking bonanza of legal troubles, whereas Grant McFadden, who fixes problems promptly and is nice, hardly generates any legal work at all.'"

—

Two lessons here: (1) If we fix problems promptly and are nice to people, we'll have fewer legal problems. (2) In the trades and professions, whether one is a plumber, a lawyer, a dentist, a roofer, or a surgeon, it is the people with problems who are going to bring in the business. Which is one of the reasons that Charlie got out of the law business.

GETTING OLDER

–

"I'm getting more experienced at aging. I'm like the man who jumped off the skyscraper and at the 5th floor on the way down says, 'So far this is not a bad ride.'"

–

Charlie has never had a prostate exam or PSA test, because he doesn't want to know if he has prostate cancer. He figures that since most men eventually have prostate problems, why worry? Nor does he worry about California earthquakes. All the things that are inevitable he refuses to worry about. That's made for an almost stress-free life and may be the reason he is now pushing ninety-three.

POSITIVE REINFORCEMENT

—

"All human beings work better when they get what psychologists call reinforcement. If you get constant rewards, even if you're Warren Buffett, you'll respond. . . . Learn from this and find out how to prosper by reinforcing the people who are close to you."

—

The secret to getting friends is to be a friend. The secret to getting help when in need is to give help to those in need. The secret to learning is to teach. The secret to getting people to excel is to reinforce their positive qualities. When the famed rock musician Bono asked Warren for help in getting the US Congress to assist his African aid project, Warren advised him to appeal not to their sympathies but to their greatness.

INCENTIVE-CAUSED BIAS

–

"You must have the confidence to override people with more credentials than you whose cognition is impaired by incentive-caused bias or some similar psychological force that is obviously present. But there are also cases where you have to recognize that you have no wisdom to add—and that your best course is to trust some expert."

–

What is incentive-caused bias? Charlie likes to tell the story of the CEO who couldn't understand why his company's newer, cheaper, and better-designed product wasn't outselling its older, more expensive model until he realized that the sales commission on the older model was higher than on the newer one. His salesmen simply made more money selling the old one. The CEO's solution was to raise the commission on the new product. Charlie recognizes that most salesmen, whether a surgical center peddling a surgery, a tire company selling tires, a real estate company selling houses, or an engineering firm selling a client on a particular design, have a money incentive driving their desire to make the sale and are predisposed to pressure you into the sale even if it is not really in your best interest. Here Charlie recommends a certain amount of skepticism and self-education to protect ourselves from being taken advantage of. Or as the playwright

INCENTIVE-CAUSED BIAS

George Bernard Shaw once said, "All professions are a conspiracy against the laity."

However, there are times when we can see the underlying biases that we need to consult an expert, in which case it is always wise to get a second opinion and sometimes even a third, and just to be on the safe side, maybe even a fourth.

NARROW-MINDEDNESS

–

"Most people are trained in one model—economics, for example—and try to solve all problems in one way. You know the saying: 'To the man with a hammer, the world looks like a nail.' This is a dumb way of handling problems."

–

This is particularly true in the field of economics, where one theory can be creating the problem that another theory is trying to solve. Take David Ricardo's economic theory of free trade, which has led to millions of American jobs being shipped overseas and is helping fuel unemployment. Keynesian economic theory says that problems of unemployment can be solved by dropping interest rates and printing money to stimulate the economy. So with one hand our government pursues an economic policy of free trade, fueling unemployment, while on the other hand the Federal Reserve is pursuing a course of lower interest rates and printing money in an effort to fight unemployment.

LIVING WELL

–

"The best armor of old age is a well-spent life preceding it."

–

This reminds me of something Warren once said to a group of college students: "We should treat our body like it is the only car we will ever own." Charlie took Warren's car analogy to heart and figured out that the less he "drove his body," the less it would wear out and the longer it would last. Which is why he is famous for avoiding any and all forms of physical exercise, other than playing bridge at the club and turning the pages of a book. What I think he is really saying is that a life spent in honorable pursuits, with an inquisitive mind, acting as part of a community, carries over into old age and leads to a very interesting and satisfying life in our later years.

MARRIAGE ADVICE

—

"In marriage, you shouldn't look for someone with good looks and character. You look for someone with low expectations."

—

A high-expectations spouse is never pleased, and you will spend your life being miserable trying to jump through hoops to please him or her. So unless you want to spend your life living with someone who is never happy, a low-expectations spouse is probably the way to go. However, the opposite is true in business: if you have low expectations for an employee or a management team, they will never rise to the occasion or learn to excel at their craft or profession. Why isn't this true for marriage? Because marriage isn't a job.

THE WORRIED RICH

—

"If you get Warren Buffett for 40 years and the bastard finally dies on you, you don't really have a right to complain."

—

This is Charlie talking about a few Berkshire Hathaway shareholders who are panicking because Charlie and Warren are getting older and the days of profiting from their brilliance are drawing to a close. There are a huge number of Berkshire shareholders who became multimillionaires under Charlie and Warren's reign, and there are even a fair number who became billionaires. Berkshire's results have been far better than anyone ever dreamed, yet there are those who are never satisfied with what life brings them, even if it's millions or billions of dollars, and who will complain about it till the very end. Francis Bacon, the sixteenth- and seventeenth-century British philosopher, scientist, and statesman, noticed a very similar phenomenon: that with some people, the richer they got, the more miserable they became—that becoming rich, for some, is more of a curse than a blessing.

THE COCA-COLA COMPANY

–

"Coke for many decades has been a basic product full of sugar, and it grew every year. Full-sugar Coke is now declining. Fortunately, the Coca-Cola Company has a vast infrastructure. Coca-Cola is declining some, but the rest of the businesses are rising. I think Coke is a strong company, and will do very well. It's still like shooting fish in a barrel."

–

The decline of Coca-Cola's full-sugar soft drinks is a favorite topic of the financial press and is the first thing that naysayers focus on when they look at Berkshire's portfolio. And it is true that sales of Coca-Cola's full-sugar drinks aren't growing as fast as they used to. However, the company owns more than five hundred different brands of sparkling and still drinks and sells 1.9 billion servings a day in more than two hundred countries. What happened at the Coca-Cola Company is that in its early days, when it was awash in cash, it went around the world buying up the most popular soft drink brands in almost every country. As the world's population increases, so does the number of Coca-Cola customers. It took forty-six years to double the world's population from 1970 to 2016, and if it takes another forty-six years to double it again, from 2016 to 2062, Coke could easily double the number of servings that it sells of all its five hundred brands. Double the number of servings that it sells, double the profit it makes. It earned $1.67 a share in 2015, so we can argue that it will make $3.34 a share in 2062, which equates to a per-share earnings growth rate of 2.17% a year. As the per-share earnings grow so will the stock price. Add in the current dividend payment of 3.24%, and we have a combined annual rate of return of 5.41%. That doesn't even consider stock buybacks increasing per-share earnings, new acquisitions, and raising the dividend, which the company has consistently done over the last thirty-nine years. In a world of negative interest rates, Coke still appears to be a tasty investment.

ENVY

—

"Well, envy and jealousy made, what, two out of the Ten Commandments? Those of you who have raised children you know about envy, or tried to run a law firm or investment bank or even a faculty? I've heard Warren say a half a dozen times, 'It's not greed that drives the world, but envy.'"

—

No stranger to the seven deadly sins, I can attest that envy and jealousy are the least enjoyable. Wrath, greed, sloth, gluttony, and lust—particularly lust—can all be great fun as one travels the self-indulgent road to disaster; however, envy and jealousy, even in small doses, will make one utterly miserable. But if Charlie and Warren are right and envy really does drive the world, it is no wonder there are so many unhappy people in it.

READING

–

"In my whole life, I have known no wise people who didn't read all the time—none, zero. You'd be amazed at how much Warren reads—and how much I read. My children laugh at me. They think I'm a book with a couple of legs sticking out."

–

Charlie has always been a voracious reader. As a child he lived in the downtown Omaha public library, where, exploring the stacks, he met the towering intellectuals of both the past and present in books; by age eight both Thomas Jefferson and Benjamin Franklin had permanent places on the bookshelf above his bed. It is reading that helped put him ahead of the pack.

TAKING THE BLOWS

–

"Life is always going to hurt some people in some ways and help others. There should be more willingness to take the blows of life as they fall. That's what manhood is, taking life as it falls. Not whining all the time and trying to fix it by whining."

–

As the great American cowboy actor John Wayne once said in a movie, "Son, I don't care much for quitters." And I expect that neither does Charlie.

USELESS WORRY

—

"I don't think it's terribly constructive to spend your time worrying about things you can't fix. As long as when you are managing your money you recognize that a terrible thing is going to happen, in the rest of your life you can be a foolish optimist."

—

As we said earlier, in the world of finance a terrible thing happens on average about once every eight to ten years. Why? Mostly because of the highly leveraged banking system. Leverage makes for huge gains as things move up but creates equally huge losses when fortunes reverse. There is also a multitude of other events that can cause the stock market to crash; the only thing anyone can be certain of is that the power of positive thinking has no place in investment decisions. As for worrying about the coming earthquake that is going to destroy the city of Los Angeles, according to Charlie, thinking about that, too, is a waste of time.

LEARNING MACHINES

—

"I constantly see people rise in life who are not the smartest, sometimes not even the most diligent, but they are learning machines. They go to bed every night a little wiser than they were when they got up, and boy, does that help, particularly when you have a long run ahead of you."

—

It is very important to be constantly learning, constantly improving ourselves. Think of it as compounding our intellect; the longer we work at it, the richer we become. It is also one of the oddities of the investment game that the older we get and the more we learn, the better investor we become. The investment field is unique. If Charlie were a surgeon, there would come a time when he just wouldn't have the physical stamina to stand fifteen hours at an operating table. The same if he were in a trade such as bricklaying. As an investor the only physical attributes he needs are his eyesight, a clear mind, and the digital dexterity to turn the pages of a book. Which is why, at ninety-two, he can still knock the ball out of the park and run circles around the new young Turks.

TRAGEDY

—

"You should never, when faced with one unbelievable tragedy, let one tragedy increase into two or three because of a failure of will."

—

This reminds me of an early Berkshire shareholder, Sam Fried, who as a teenage boy in Europe survived the horrors of Auschwitz by sheer willpower, came to Omaha after the war, created a beautiful family and an amazing business, became one of the leading elders in the community, and along the way enriched a great many lives with his love and generosity.

MULTITASKING

–

"I think people who multitask pay a huge price."

–

Many people believe that when they multitask, they are being superproductive. Charlie believes that if you don't have time to think about something deeply, you are giving your competitors, who are thinking deeply, a great advantage over you. Charlie's ability to focus intensely and really think about something has been his competitive edge in beating Wall Street at its own game.

FELICITY

—

"They once asked me what one person accounted for most of my personal felicity in life, and I said, 'That's easy—that would be my wife's first husband.'"

—

Felicity—intense happiness—this is Charlie's clever way of saying that his second wife, Nancy, brought him great happiness. I think it's also his way of saying that her expectations were brought down very low by man number one.

HEALTH

–

"I eat whatever I want to eat. I have never paid any attention to my health. I've never done any exercise I didn't want to do. If any success has come to me, it came because I insisted on thinking things through . . . all these people who think they are going to get ahead by jogging or something, more power to them."

–

Since Charlie is ninety-two and in great physical and mental health, there might be something to this "thinking" form of exercise. He does belong to a country club, but, as we said, he spends most of his time in the card room playing bridge. I guess shuffling cards could be counted as a form of exercise.

A SEAMLESS WEB

–

"The highest form that civilization can reach is a seamless web of deserved trust—not much procedure, just totally reliable people correctly trusting one another. . . . In your own life what you want is a seamless web of deserved trust. And if your proposed marriage contract has forty-seven pages, I suggest you not enter."

–

Charlie and Warren often quote the twentieth-century Omaha construction titan Peter Kiewit, who once said that he wanted to hire people who were smart, hardworking, and honest. But out of the three, honesty was the most important, because if they weren't honest, the two other qualities, smart and hardworking, were going to steal him blind. The corporate culture at Berkshire is that if you can't trust someone, you really shouldn't be doing business with him or her. On the topic of marriage, Charlie has always said that we shouldn't be timid about getting married when we find the right spouse. I guess a forty-seven-page marriage contract might indicate that we still haven't found the love of our life.

MISSED CHANCES

—

"I think the attitude of Epictetus is the best. He thought that every missed chance in life was an opportunity to behave well, every missed chance in life was an opportunity to learn something, and that your duty was not to be submerged in self-pity, but to utilize the terrible blow in constructive fashion. That is a very good idea."

—

The Greek Stoic philosopher Epictetus, who lived A.D. 55–135, started life as a slave to the secretary of Emperor Nero in Rome. He studied philosophy and on Nero's death was made a freeman. He then taught philosophy in Rome till Emperor Domitian banished all philosophers from the city, whereupon he fled back to Greece and started his own school of philosophy.

Epictetus taught that philosophy is a way of life—that all external events are determined by fate and are beyond our control. But as individuals we are responsible for our own actions. The financial parallel to "Epictetus's fate" is the macro- and microeconomic events that affect individual companies and their corresponding rising and falling stock prices. How we respond to those events, whether or not we learn from them, is our own responsibility.

In Charlie's investment life each and every loss has been a learning lesson. If he had never experienced troubles with a business in very competitive industries—textiles, shoes, retail clothing, and airlines—he might never have gained the insight into the wonders of owning a business that had a consumer monopoly such as Coca-Cola or See's Candies. He would never have seen how a low-cost producer such as GEICO can have a competitive advantage over its much bigger competitors. If he had never experienced the pain of the market crash of 1973–74, he never would have had the foresight to stockpile the cash he used to buy Wells Fargo stock in 2008–09. Thomas Edison once said, "I failed my way to success." Though Charlie never experienced as many failures as Edison did, he can still credit his early failures as the source of much of his success.

LYING TO ONESELF

—

"Dean Kendall of the University of Michigan music school once told me a story: 'When I was a little boy, I was put in charge of a little retail operation that included candy. My father saw me take a piece of candy and eat it. I said, "Don't worry. I intend to replace it." My father said, "That sort of thinking will ruin your mind. It will be much better for you if you take all you want and call yourself a thief every time you do it."'"

—

The French philosopher Jean-Paul Sartre called lying to oneself an act of "bad faith" because it negated "truth," which would destroy not only the moral fiber of the individual but also the society in which we live. Why society? Because, as Sartre argued in the smoke-filled cafés of 1940s Paris, we can't build a successful civilization on a bed of half-truths and lies. Here Charlie is saying that the little lies that people tell themselves to justify their bad acts can often grow into bigger lies that will destroy not only their lives but also the lives of many others—as in 2007–09, when the "bad faith" acts of the nefarious denizens of Wall Street nearly destroyed much of the world's economy.

TRUTH

—

"Remember Louis Vincenti's rule: 'Tell the truth, and you won't have to remember your lies.'"

—

Louis Vincenti was an attorney and the much-respected chairman and chief executive officer of Wesco Financial Corporation until retiring at age seventy-seven. He was well known for having a brilliant business mind and being direct and to the point. He called it like it was and always told the truth. It is said he was the embodiment of integrity and a huge influence on both Charlie and Warren.

PERSPECTIVE

—

"It's bad to have an opinion you're proud of if you can't state the arguments for the other side better than your opponents. This is a great mental discipline."

—

This mental exercise comes from Charlie's early training in law, where it is an advantage to be able to argue both sides of a case. Knowing the other side's arguments, its possible points of attack, allows one to prepare counterattacks long before a case gets into the courtroom. The most interesting thing about this mental exercise is that after learning the other side's arguments we just might discover that they are right and we were wrong. Which is probably why so few people take Charlie's advice on this.

MULTIDISCIPLINE

–

"If you have enough sense to become a mental adult yourself, you can run rings around people smarter than you. Just pick up key ideas from all the disciplines, not just a few, and you're immensely wiser than they are."

–

A man who can play all the instruments in an orchestra can write a symphony, but a man who can play only the viola, even if he is the greatest viola player on earth, can play only the viola. Charlie is a man who can discuss Charles Darwin's thoughts on evolution, Stephen Jay Gould's thoughts on Darwin's thoughts, Albert Einstein's unified field theory, Walter Bagehot's 1873 treatise on central banking, Isaac Newton and Gottfried Wilhelm Leibniz's development of calculus, Marcia Stigum's voluminous work on the money market, Marquis and Jessie R. James's history of the Bank of America, the conflict between Robert Oppenheimer and Edward Teller over the development of the hydrogen bomb, and E. O. Wilson's theories of sociobiology all in the same breath. He can even quote Mark Twain and Immanuel Kant when the occasion calls for it. Though he is not as well versed in the areas of twentieth-century German Expressionist theater, Dadaism, and Diaghilev's Ballets Russes, he makes up for it by knowing a hell of a lot about how to make money in the stock market. I might add that he is also knowledgeable about some of the more important things in life, such as fishing for walleye in the lakes of Minnesota.

CIVILIZATION

—

"Over the long term, the eclipse rate of great civilizations being overtaken is 100%. So you know how it's going to end."

—

From the ninth to twelfth centuries Venice was the financial and business center of the world, and even though those days have long since passed, Venice is still a very wealthy city and Venetians are still considered to be some of the most successful entrepreneurs and businesspeople in Europe. Just because you aren't number one anymore doesn't mean you can't make a ton of money as number two. If you don't believe me, just look at Charlie; he has been the number two man at Berkshire Hathaway since 1979, and he hasn't done too shabbily.

REFLECTION

—

"I like you all because you remind me of myself. Who doesn't like his own image staring back at him?"

—

The magic mirror is always at work. We like you, too! And thank you, Charlie, for all the wonderful gifts of knowledge that you have shared with us over the years!

ACKNOWLEDGMENTS

I wish to thank Kate, Dexter, and Miranda for their infinite patience and love. And a special thank-you to my amazing publisher and editor, Roz Lippel, at Scribner for giving me the opportunity to think and write about interesting people and some very esoteric subjects. I would also like to thank my very dear friend and mentor Wyoming attorney Gerry Spence, who taught me how to fight for justice. And last but not least, I'd like to thank Warren Buffett for bringing into my life the wonderful and fascinating Charlie Munger.

SOURCES

1. Daily Journal Annual Meeting, 2015, http://www.forbes.com/sites/phildemuth/2015/04/20/charlie-mungers-2015-daily-journal-annual-meeting-part-3/#20f8719d6f0e

2. http://blogs.wsj.com/moneybeat/2014/09/12/a-fireside-chat-with-charlie-munger/

3. Daily Journal Annual Meeting, 2015, http://www.forbes.com/sites/phildemuth/2015/04/13/charlie-mungers-2015-daily-journal-annual-meeting-part-2/#429049264673

4. http://www.gurufocus.com/news/144211/charlie-mungers-wisdom-poker-and-votes

5. Daily Journal Annual Meeting, 2015, http://www.forbes.com/sites/phildemuth/2015/04/07/charlie-mungers-2015-daily-journal-annual-meeting-part-1/#39be30b31d62

6. https://old.ycombinator.com/munger.html

7. http://blogs.wsj.com/moneybeat/2014/09/12/a-fireside-chat-with-charlie-munger/

8. http://www.quoteswise.com/investing-quotes.html

9. http://www.thepracticalway.com/2010/12/20/quotes-charlie-munger/

SOURCES

10. http://www.nexusinvestments.com/the-wit-and-wisdom-of -charlie-munger/

11. Tren Griffin, *Charlie Munger: The Complete Investor* (New York: Columbia University Press, 2015), p. 129.

12. Wesco Annual Meeting, 2006, http://www.valueplays.net/ wp-content/uploads/The-Best-of-Charlie-Munger-1994-2011 .pdf

13. http://www.jameslau88.com/charlie_munger_on_checklist_ investing.htm

14. http://www.thepracticalway.com/2010/12/20/quotes-charlie -munger/

15. Daily Journal Annual Meeting, 2016, http://thecharlieton.com/ the-2016-daily-journal-meetings-notes-february-10-2016/

16. Berkshire Hathaway Annual Meeting, 2001, http://www.ben grahaminvesting.ca/Resources/Books/The-Best-of-Charlie -Munger-1994-2011.pdf

17. Daily Journal Meeting, 2015, http://www.marketfolly. com/2015/03/notes-from-charlie-mungers-daily.html

18. Wesco Annual Meeting, 2006, http://www.valueplays.net/wp -content/uploads/The-Best-of-Charlie-Munger-1994-2011.pdf

19. Daily Journal Annual Meeting, 2015, http://www.forbes.com/ sites/phildemuth/2015/04/07/charlie-mungers-2015-daily -journal-annual-meeting-part-1/#39be30b31d62

20. Griffin, *Charlie Munger*, p. 39

21. Berkshire Annual Meeting, 2003, http://www.fool.com/ news/2003/05/05/report-from-berkshires-meeting.aspx

SOURCES

22. Berkshire Annual Meeting, 2005, http://www.tilsonfunds.com/brkmtg05notes.pdf

23. http://www.philanthropyroundtable.org/topic/excellence_in_philanthropy/masters_class

24. http://blogs.wsj.com/moneybeat/2014/09/12/a-fireside-chat-with-charlie-munger/

25. http://blogs.wsj.com/moneybeat/2014/09/12/the-secrets-of-berkshire-hathaways-success-an-interview-with-charlie-munger/

26. https://old.ycombinator.com/munger.html

27. Daily Journal Annual Meeting, 2015, http://www.forbes.com/sites/phildemuth/2015/04/20/charlie-mungers-2015-daily-journal-annual-meeting-part-3/#20f8719d6f0e

28. Daily Journal Annual Meeting, 2015, http://www.forbes.com/sites/phildemuth/2015/04/07/charlie-mungers-2015-daily-journal-annual-meeting-part-1/#39be30b31d62

29. http://today.law.harvard.edu/feature/money/

30. Berkshire Hathaway Annual Meeting, 2000, http://www.fool.com/investing/general/2015/01/17/12-of-the-best-things-charlie-munger-has-ever-said.aspx

31. Bud Labitan, *The Four Filters Invention of Warren Buffett and Charlie Munger*, p. 79

32. http://www.jameslau88.com/charlie_munger_on_the_conventional_wisdom_on_foundation_investing.htm

33. Wesco Annual Meeting, 1989, from Janet Lowe, *Damn Right! Behind the Scenes with Berkshire Hathaway Billionaire Charlie Munger* (Hoboken, NJ: Wiley, 2003), p. 150

SOURCES

34. https://old.ycombinator.com/munger.html

35. Daily Journal Annual Meeting, 2014, http://www.jianshu.com/p/4be97742ef5b

36. Daily Journal Annual Meeting, 2014, http://www.jianshu.com/p/4be97742ef5b

37. Berkshire Annual Meeting, 2015, http://www.businessinsider.com/warren-buffett-charlie-munger-quotes-at-berkshire-hathaway-annual-meeting-2015-5

38. Daily Journal Annual Meeting, 2014, http://theinvestmentsblog.blogspot.com/2015/05/berkshires-architect.html

39. Wesco Annual Meeting, 2002, http://www.jameslau88.com/charlie_munger_at_the_2002_wesco_annual_meeting.htm

40. Wesco Annual Meeting, 2009, http://www.valuewalk.com/wp-content/uploads/2014/05/Charlie-Munger-2005-2013-minus-Harvard-Westlake.pdf

41. Daily Journal Annual Meeting, 2014, http://www.jianshu.com/p/4be97742ef5b

42. Daily Journal Meeting, 2016, http://www.valuewalk.com/2016/02/charlie-munger-daily-journal-2016/?all=1

43. Wesco Annual Meeting, 2009, http://www.bengrahaminvesting.ca/Resources/Books/The-Best-of-Charlie-Munger-1994-2011.pdf

44. https://old.ycombinator.com/munger.html

45. http://blogs.wsj.com/moneybeat/2014/09/12/the-secrets-of-berkshire-hathaways-success-an-interview-with-charlie-munger/

46. Wesco Annual Meeting, 2009, http://www.valuewalk.com/wp-content/uploads/2014/05/Charlie-Munger-2005-2013-minus-Harvard-Westlake.pdf

47. Berkshire Annual Meeting, 2006, http://www.fool.com/news/2003/05/05/report-from-berkshires-meeting.aspx

48. Wesco Annual Meeting, 2011, Questions and Answers, http://www.fool.com/investing/general/2012/06/14/charlie-mungers-30-best-zingers-of-all-time.aspx

49. Wesco Annual Meeting, 2010, http://www.fool.com/investing/value/2010/05/07/charlie-mungers-thoughts-on-just-about-everything.aspx

50. Berkshire Annual Meeting, 2002, http://www.azquotes.com/author/20634-Charlie_Munger/tag/capitalism

51. Wesco Annual Meeting, 2005, http://www.tilsonfunds.com/wscmtg05notes.pdf

52. http://thecharlieton.com/category/hedgefundnotes/

53. Wesco Annual Meeting, 2009, http://www.fool.com/investing/value/2009/05/08/charlie-mungers-thoughts-on-just-about-everything.aspx

54. http://money.cnn.com/2005/05/01/news/fortune500/buffett_talks/index.htm

55. Wesco Annual Meeting, 2002, http://www.jameslau88.com/charlie_munger_at_the_2002_wesco_annual_meeting.htm

56. Wesco Annual Meeting, 2004, http://mungerisms.blogspot.com/2009/10/wesco-2004-annual-meeting.html

57. Wesco Annual Meeting, 2009, http://www.fool.com/investing/
value/2009/05/08/charlie-mungers-thoughts-on-just-about
-everything.aspx

58. Daily Journal Annual Meeting, 2015, http://www.forbes.com/
sites/phildemuth/2015/04/20/charlie-mungers-2015-daily
-journal-annual-meeting-part-3/#20f8719d6f0e

59. Daily Journal Annual Meeting, 2015, http://www.forbes.com/
sites/phildemuth/2015/04/07/charlie-mungers-2015-daily
-journal-annual-meeting-part-1/#39be30b31d62

60. Daily Journal Annual Meeting, 2015, http://www.forbes.com/
sites/phildemuth/2015/04/07/charlie-mungers-2015-daily
-journal-annual-meeting-part-1/#39be30b31d62

61. http://www.cnbc.com/id/100705820

62. Daily Journal Annual Meeting, 2014, http://www.jianshu
.com/p/4be97742ef5b

63. Wesco Annual Meeting, 2005, http://www.bengrahaminvesting
.ca/Resources/Books/The-Best-of-Charlie-Munger-1994-2011
.pdf

64. Wesco Annual Meeting, 2009, http://docslide.us/documents/
wesco-financial-meeting-notes-1999-2009.html

65. Daily Journal Annual Meeting, 2014, http://www.forbes.com/
sites/phildemuth/2014/09/25/charlie-munger-and-the-2014
-daily-journal-annual-meeting-part-two/#77dc5b3f3b71

66. Daily Journal Annual Meeting, 2015, http://www.forbes.com/
sites/phildemuth/2015/04/20/charlie-mungers-2015-daily
-journal-annual-meeting-part-3/#20f8719d6f0e

SOURCES

67. Daily Journal Annual Meeting, 2014, http://www.jianshu
    .com/p/4be97742ef5b

68. Daily Journal Annual Meeting, 2014, http://www.jianshu
    .com/p/4be97742ef5b

69. Daily Journal Annual Meeting, 2014, http://www.jianshu
    .com/p/4be97742ef5b

70. http://today.law.harvard.edu/feature/money/

71. Berkshire Hathaway Annual Meeting, May 2000, from Alice
    Schroeder, *The Snowball: Warren Buffett and the Business of Life*
    (New York: Bantam, 2008), p. 579

72. http://www.thepracticalway.com/2010/12/20/quotes-charlie-munger/

73. http://www.thepracticalway.com/2010/12/20/quotes-charlie
    -munger/

74. http://theinvestmentsblog.blogspot.com/2011/06/munger-two
    -kinds-of-businesses-part-ii.html

75. http://www.thepracticalway.com/2010/12/20/quotes-charlie
    -munger/

76. http://theinvestmentsblog.blogspot.com/2013/06/buffett-and
    -munger-on-sees-candy.html

77. Lowe, Damn Right, p. 150

78. Interview with the BBC, 2009, http://www.psyfitec.com/2009/10/
    buffett-and-munger-on-bbc.html

79. https://old.ycombinator.com/munger.html

80. https://old.ycombinator.com/munger.html

81. Wesco Annual Meeting, 2005, http://www.tilsonfunds.com/
    wscmtg05notes.pdf

82. Wesco Annual Meeting, 2005, http://www.tilsonfunds.com/
    wscmtg05notes.pdf

83. Wesco Annual Meeting, 2003, https://variantperceptions.word
    press.com/category/munger/

84. Wesco Annual Meeting, 2008, mungerisms.blogspot
    .com/2009/08/2008-annual-meeting-notes.html

85. Wesco Annual Meeting, 2007, http://www.valuewalk.com/
    wp-content/uploads/2014/05/Charlie-Munger-2005-2013
    -minus-Harvard-Westlake.pdf

86. http://thecharlieton.com/category/hedgefundnotes/

87. Wesco Annual Meeting, 2007, http://www.bengrahaminvesting
    .ca/Resources/Books/The-Best-of-Charlie-Munger-1994-2011
    .pdf

88. Wesco Annual Meeting, 2010, http://www.bengrahaminvesting
    .ca/Resources/Books/The-Best-of-Charlie-Munger-1994-2011
    .pdf

89. Wesco Annual Meeting, 2005, http://www.tilsonfunds.com/
    wscmtg05notes.pdf

90. Wesco Annual Meeting, 2008, http://www.bengrahaminvesting
    .ca/Resources/Books/The-Best-of-Charlie-Munger-1994-2011.pdf

91. Wesco Annual Meeting, 2007, http://www.bengrahaminvesting
    .ca/Resources/Books/The-Best-of-Charlie-Munger-1994-2011
    .pdf

92. http://www.thepracticalway.com/2010/12/20/quotes-charlie
    -munger/

SOURCES

93. http://www.quoteswise.com/charlie-munger-quotes-4.html

94. Griffin, *Charlie Munger*, p. 42

95. http://www.gurufocus.com/news/119820/30-of-charlie-mungers-best-quotes

96. Griffin, *Charlie Munger*, p. 85

97. Wesco Annual Meeting, 2010, http://www.fool.com/investing/value/2010/05/07/charlie-mungers-thoughts-on-just-about-everything.aspx

98. Berkshire Hathaway Annual Meeting, 2011, http://www.fool.com/investing/general/2011/07/05/charlie-mungers-thoughts-on-the-world-part-2.aspx

99. http://boundedrationality.wordpress.com/quotes/charlie-munger/

100. Daily Journal Annual Meeting, 2015, http://www.gurufocus.com/news/394902/seeking-wisdom-from-charlie-munger

101. http://www.valueinvestingworld.com/2014/10/charlie-munger-on-how-he-invested-when.html

102. Wesco Annual Meeting, 2007, http://www.valuewalk.com/wp-content/uploads/2014/05/Charlie-Munger-2005-2013-minus-Harvard-Westlake.pdf

103. http://www.thepracticalway.com/2010/12/20/quotes-charlie-munger/

104. Berkshire Annual Meeting, 2015, http://www.businessinsider.com/warren-buffett-charlie-munger-quotes-at-berkshire-hathaway-annual-meeting-2015-5

SOURCES

105. Daily Journal Annual Meeting, 2014, http://www.forbes.com/
     sites/phildemuth/2014/10/08/charlie-munger-and-the-2014
     -daily-journal-annual-meeting-part-four/#1bef4833644b
106. http://www.talkativeman.com/mungerisms-charlie-mungers
     -100-best-zingers-of-all-time/
107. http://genius.com/Charlie-munger-usc-law-commencement
     -speech-annotated
108. Wesco Annual Meeting, 2006, Question and Answers, https://
     www.goodreads.com/quotes/12934-we-all-are-learning
     -modifying-or-destroying-ideas-all-the
109. Daily Journal Annual Meeting, 2015, http://www.forbes.com/
     sites/phildemuth/2015/04/20/charlie-mungers-2015-daily
     -journal-annual-meeting-part-3/#20f8719d6f0e
110. https://www.gsb.stanford.edu/sites/default/files/38_Munger_0
     .pdf
111. Wesco Annual Meeting, 2007, http://www.fool.com/investing/
     general/2014/09/07/warren-buffetts-right-hand-man-reveals
     -his-secrets.aspx
112. Wesco Annual Meeting, 2007, http://www.bengrahaminvesting
     .ca/Resources/Books/The-Best-of-Charlie-Munger-1994-2011
     .pdf
113. Wesco Annual Meeting, 2009, http://www.bengrahaminvesting
     .ca/Resources/Books/The-Best-of-Charlie-Munger-1994-2011
     .pdf
114. Wesco Annual Meeting, 2007, http://www.bengrahaminvesting
     .ca/Resources/Books/The-Best-of-Charlie-Munger-1994-2011.pdf

115. Wesco Annual Meeting, 2007, http://www.bengrahaminvesting
.ca/Resources/Books/The-Best-of-Charlie-Munger-1994-2011
.pdf

116. https://truinn.wordpress.com/2014/04/30/wisdom-from-charlie
-munger-i/

117. Griffin, *Charlie Munger*, p. 42

118. Charles T. Munger, *Poor Charlie's Almanac: The Wit and Wisdom
of Charles T. Munger*, https://www.goodreads.com/author/
quotes/236437.Charles_T_Munger

119. Daily Journal Annual Meeting, 2015, http://www.bedelfinancial
.com/blog/elaines-blog/warren-buffett-and-charlie-munger
-more-than-investing/289/

120. Wesco Annual Meeting, 2007, http://www.fool.com/investing/
general/2009/05/04/roundtable-buffetts-biggest-berkshire-bomb.aspx

121. http://latticeworkinvesting.com/2016/02/13/charlie-munger
-transcript-of-daily-journal-annual-meeting-2016/

122. http://www.rbcpa.com/mungerspeech_june_95.pdf

123. http://www.quoteswise.com/charlie-munger-quotes-2.html

124. Daily Journal Annual Meeting, 2015, http://www.forbes.com/
sites/phildemuth/2015/04/20/charlie-mungers-2015-daily
-journal-annual-meeting-part-3/#20f8719d6f0e

125. Daily Journal Annual Meeting, 2015, http://www.forbes.com/
sites/phildemuth/2015/04/20/charlie-mungers-2015-daily
-journal-annual-meeting-part-3/#20f8719d6f0e

126. http://genius.com/Charlie-munger-usc-law-commencement
-speech-annotated

127. Schroeder, *Snowball*, p. 198

128. Daily Journal Annual Meeting, 2015, http://www.forbes.com/
sites/phildemuth/2015/04/07/charlie-mungers-2015-daily
-journal-annual-meeting-part-1/#39be30b31d62

129. Daily Journal Annual Meeting, 2014, http://www.forbes.com/
sites/phildemuth/2014/09/19/charlie-munger-and-the-2014
-daily-journal-annual-meeting-a-fans-notes/#478bb4387384

130. Daily Journal Annual Meeting, 2015, http://www.forbes.com/
sites/phildemuth/2015/04/07/charlie-mungers-2015-daily
-journal-annual-meeting-part-1/#39be30b31d62

131. https://www.gsb.stanford.edu/sites/default/files/38_Munger_0
.pdf

132. http://genius.com/Charlie-munger-usc-law-commencement
-speech-annotated

133. Wesco Annual Meeting, 2007, http://www.bengrahaminvesting
.ca/Resources/Books/The-Best-of-Charlie-Munger-1994-2011
.pdf

134. Wesco Annual Meeting, 2004, http://www.bengrahaminvesting
.ca/Resources/Books/The-Best-of-Charlie-Munger-1994-2011
.pdf

135. Wesco Annual Meeting, 2006, http://www.bengrahaminvesting
.ca/Resources/Books/The-Best-of-Charlie-Munger-1994-2011
.pdf

136. Wesco Annual Meeting, 2007, http://www.bengrahaminvesting
.ca/Resources/Books/The-Best-of-Charlie-Munger-1994-2011
.pdf

SOURCES

137. Wesco Annual Meeting, 2005, http://www.bengrahaminvesting
.ca/Resources/Books/The-Best-of-Charlie-Munger-1994-2011
.pdf

138. Daily Journal Annual Meeting, 2014, http://www.jianshu
.com/p/4be97742ef5b

INDEX

INDEX

INDEX

INDEX

INDEX

investing (*cont.*)

evaluating new technology in, 81–82

figuring out worth of company before, 22–23, 39, 58, 67

financial companies in, 42–43

financial incentives for ratings companies and, 26

finding underpriced stocks after a market panic, 19

fixing problems promptly and, 181

focusing skills in, 38

forecasts and predictions not useful in, 32

Graham's philosophy on, 20, 22–23

"great business at a fair price" approach in, 125–26

holding investments in, 48–49, 56–57

idea destruction thought process in, 175–76

ideology in, 174

inflation and, 100–101

investment managers and, 46–47

keeping large cash balances ready for, 35, 38, 62, 65, 72, 75, 82

knowing what you don't know about, 16, 25, 162

knowing when to buy heavily in, 30

knowing when to sell and walk away in, 18

learning continually as part of, 179, 196

learning from failures in, 164, 202–3

learning from mistakes in, 165

lessons from bad businesses owned in, 131

for the long term. *See* long-term investing

making mistakes in, 165

management of banks invested in and, 77

margin of safety in, 22–23, 53

mergers and, 122

mispriced gambles in, 27–28

no simple, single formula in, 78–79

not being an idiot in, 17

not being stupid in, 61

overconfidence and, 44–45

as ownership of fractional interest in a business, 58–59

patience in, 32, 38, 69–71, 82

positioning in late bull markets and, 65–66

preventing unfavorable surprises in, 53

psychology and, 159

recognizing economic reality of companies in, 60

Rembrandt prices analogy in, 39, 40

INDEX

INDEX

INDEX

ABOUT THE AUTHOR

For more than twenty years David Clark has been considered one of the world's leading authorities on the subject of Warren Buffett's investment methods. His international bestselling investment books, coauthored with Mary Buffett, have been translated into more than twenty foreign languages and are considered "investment classics" the world over. He holds a BS degree in finance and a law degree from the University of California, Hastings College of the Law. When not consumed with matters of finance, he is engaged in the second great passion of his life, which is trial law, and maintains an active national practice.